"Becoming a parent is easily the greatest challenge that we will ever face. There are no handbooks or guides that give us magic answers to the huge questions that we are bombarded with. Lindsey's faith is an inspiration to us all. She is wise beyond her age."

Joe LaChance

"Brooklyn made the biggest impact on my life, and in turn others, when I read she needed credits for blood. I now donate every chance I get."

Gerad Caldwell

"Brooklyn is a constant inspiration to me. This disease is awful, so awful. Some days I can't get my muscles to work well enough for me to speak. I often think of Brooklyn and her not being able to make sounds of pain or hunger. She shows so much determination and strength, and inspires me on a daily basis."

Alisa Turner (Victim of Lyme's disease)

"Anytime I am down or having a hard time about how long my waiting process is going, I am reminded of little Brooklyn and how I can SEE God working, it about knocks me off my feet every time."

Ally Pichnic

"Watching Lindsey document each movement and each miracle truly brought the real spirit of the holidays into perspective for me. Her faith seems unending and that is beautiful."

Erin McCann

"In all my life I have read and witnessed countless stories of how a Faithful God meets His children in their most desperate times of need. And in all my life I have never seen His faithfulness revealed more clearly than through the life of a sweet little girl named Brooklyn. I watched as Brooklyn's daily battles became God's anthem of power and a constant reminder that He is always working through the smallest things to get our attention. God is always faithful and Brooklyn's life is the perfect and shining example that stands on behalf of His Faithfulness!"

Blair Marsh

Surviving
C47

Surviving
C47

A story of hope, faith,
and a girl named Brooklyn

LINDSEY HALES

LUCIDBOOKS

For Brooklyn

Contents

Preface

At week 20 in my pregnancy, our child was diagnosed with a Congenital Diaphragmatic Hernia. We were told there was a hole in her diaphragm, and that her intestines were crowding her chest. She would undergo surgery at birth, and face many trials in order to survive. My husband and I were scared, but we clung to our faith and believed that God had placed this little girl in our lives for a reason.

I had begun an online blog shortly after my husband and I were married. It started as a humorous twist to the struggles and triumphs after "I Do". My writings took a sharp turn when we found out about our little girl and her diagnosis. From that day on, the blog has served as a source of information to Brooklyn's many supporters. These posts were all originally typed on an iPhone, and then posted via tumblr, on my blog site. The medical terminology presented in this book is not claimed to be accurate or correct. I, as a Mother, took what the doctors provided us each day, and interpreted the information to the best of my abilities and knowledge. There was no further research involved in my posts. All facts were gathered from the daily discussions her doctors had when meeting at Brooklyn's bedside. These writings bear raw emotion, and the religious journey I took whilst Brooklyn fought for her life. They reflect a glimpse into the hope and fears of our family's experience. I feel that Brooklyn's story reaches out to anyone who has ever questioned "why?" No matter what battle you face in life, Brooklyn's perseverance is purely encouraging. I am honored to share her story, but feel it necessary to prepare readers for a somewhat patchy work of literature. I do not claim to be an expert writer, nor do I feel this book is perfect. I wrote because it was an outlet. I was able to release the pressure I felt daily from life in the hospital.

Brooklyn Elizabeth Hales was born on November 28th, 2010. She was the most beautiful thing we had ever witnessed. Without a chance to hold her in my arms, she was whisked away to the NICU at Texas Children's Hospital in Houston, Texas. Hooked to tubes and wires, our little girl was struggling to hold on. Over the next few days, she fell in and out of stability. Her vitals jumped up and down as the doctors worked hard to control her treatment.

We took it one day at a time.

Brooklyn has proven herself a fighter and has touched the hearts of many. We will forever be indebted to the family, friends, and medical staff who originally followed her story and remain faithful to this day. Our family was blessed to have an overwhelming support group. Brooklyn continues to amaze us with her endurance, and we are grateful for the honor to be her parents. She has taught us all to "have a little faith", and I encourage you to learn from her journey.

Lindsey Hales

August 9th, 2010

Starbucks isn't meant to make you cry. On the contrary, the amount of caffeine shooting through your veins should ultimately send your body into a state of elated shock. The rush should ignite your senses, leaving you with a jump start to your morning. Starbucks, for some, is the glue holding life's pieces together. Yet here I sit; tall passion ice tea in one hand, banana nut loaf in the other, broken.

Friday was going to be a day of celebration. We were to find out if the baby I was carrying was a boy or girl, and then call everyone we knew to spread the news. It didn't go quite as planned, as life usually doesn't. After finding out our little munchkin was a girl, we were filled with so much joy. Smiles on our faces, we finally felt the reality of parenthood set in. The excitement was cut short, however, when the ultrasound technician said she had some concerns. Leaving the room to get the doctor, we were left with worry of the unknown. Worst case scenarios flooded our thoughts as attempts to block out fear failed. My husband pulled me close and said a simple prayer. Our hearts were sober as the news bemused our ears like an unknown dialect. The doctor returned and told us that our baby girl has what is known as a Congenital Diaphragmatic Hernia (CDH). Her diaphragm did not develop fully and had left a small hole. Some of her intestines were now in the chest cavity, crowding her lungs and causing her heart to be pushed to the other side of her body. The words sank heavy on our wounded spirits. This was not what we had come for. At the end of my examination, the doctor ushered us into a small conference room down the hall. A few minutes seemed more like hours as we waited patiently for the genetics counselor. My body hurt with emotion. My breathing was shallow as the tiny hairs of my arms stood tall. The back of my mind raced with the terror of the doctors suggesting termination. There was no budging my stance; I was going to remain faithful to my pregnancy and our daughter. Nothing could shake my decision to keep this gift God had created. Whatever the outcome, I would walk boldly with confidence.

A knock on the door jolted me from my trance. Entering the room was a petite woman with a pixie cut. Her grace and stature mimicked that of Tinkerbelle. If only she had brought with her some fairy dust to make this day disappear. The counselor did her best to lay out the details of our daughter's diagnosis. Big words flew about the room as I tried desperately to hold on to their meaning. Slipping through my ears, her voice was distant. The diagrams she laid in front of us were like ink blots, unrecognizable and foreign. I wanted to grasp what she was trying to say, but at the same time I was tuning her out. I didn't want to hear that CDH can be genetic. I refused to hear about the missing chromosome and the term "failure to thrive". Thirty minutes flew by and we were given the choice to do a genetic test. This would rule out the darkest outcome and inform us of the extent to our daughter's prognosis. After discussing our options, we decided to do the amniocentesis to make sure it was not a genetic disorder. In my heart I knew it wasn't, but I wanted the doctors to have all the information necessary. They needed to know every detail of our sweet girl so that they would be ready for anything. I am a firm believer that every shred of evidence is essential to solving a crime. The doctors would not have the excuse of missing pieces to this puzzle. Back in the exam room, I laid silently on the table. The needle was big, but God was bigger. The results were negative. Our daughter's chromosomal make up was perfect. This hole happened by chance and the worst case scenario was denied access. One hurdle down.

We now wait until next Tuesday where we will spend the majority of the day having an MRI and Echocardiograph done on our daughter. We will be able to speak with a pediatric surgeon about how serious her condition is and what steps will be taken along the way. We have been praying daily for a miracle. We know that she is in God's hands, the perfect place to be. We want to amaze the doctor's with his ability to heal by the power of prayer. Nothing is too difficult or out of reach for our Lord. He is all knowing, all powerful, and can handle anything. It is only our doubts that weaken his action. We must remain faithful that He succeeds. All we have to do is ask out of faith and it will be given. He has already promised to never leave us or forsake us. If we are obedient, he will prevail. This is why we know that our girl will be just fine. For now, we remain steadfast in prayer, keeping our faith in the name of Jesus. He has said what is asked shall be given, and we are asking for him to heal our baby girl.

I am crying in the line at Starbucks because God has shown himself in this dark hour. Pulling up to the drive thru window, the lady in green smiled at me. With a sweet voice she informed me that the person in front of me paid for my treats. This small gesture sent me over the edge. It was as if God was reminding me that everything was going to be ok. That His plan was bigger than my pain, and He would see me through this.

What's in a Name

I hadn't thought much about our daughter's name. I knew that regardless of her first, Elizabeth would be her middle. It is a family name on both sides, and it's strong. Very 1800's, but classic. We had debated for weeks on her first name. I'll admit the choosing process was much harder than I had expected. Boy names came particularly easy for some reason. We had a list the size of Santa's full of them. However, girl's names escaped us. If I liked one, my husband would veto it, and vice versa. We were unable to find mutual love for one. We wanted something unique but not quite "new age" like "Apple". No offense to Gwyneth Paltrow, we just weren't into fruit or seasons. "Summer" was not among the top ten.

Then came "Brooklyn" in a random conversation.

It was everything we wanted. Different, but not over the top. Sweet, but strong. Bold and beautiful. Once we found it, there was no turning back.

Before we knew the gender, it was hard not to call the baby "it". To say "him or her" in every spot was exhausting, and I found myself losing focus when having to do this. My best friend Madeline had a solution to our problem. She suggested we come up with a gender neutral name until we found out blue or pink. I respected this idea and became interested to see what she had in mind. After a five second pause she suggested, "Herbie". I loved it. From that moment until week 20, Brooklyn's name was Herbie. Our family and friends had fun poking at the name, and if you knew Madeline, it was that much more entertaining. One of the reasons I love her so much is that she can laugh at her own joke when no one else does. She was the perfect candidate to label our "it" baby.

This morning while I was changing the Facebook photo album name from "Herbie" to "Brooklyn", I got curious as to the origin or meaning of the name. I was overwhelmed with emotion at my findings.

<u>Brooklyn</u>: means water, or stream.
and
<u>Elizabeth</u>: means My God is bountiful; God of Plenty.

Both of these hit me immediately and I started to look up scripture on how water was used in the bible. Of course we know that it was used in his healings on the Sabbath at the pool of Bethesda. We also see it used earlier in the Book of John where it states, "but whosoever drinks of the water that I will give him will never be thirsty again. The water that I give him will become in him a spring of water welling up to eternal life". It's also seen in the very beginning when God was creating life on Earth: "In Genesis 1:20, we read of the first mention of life, and this life comes from water, "…Let the waters bring forth abundantly the moving creature that hath life…""

Even this would be enough to know that our God is with Brooklyn. But we also have Elizabeth which means "My God is bountiful". He is God of plenty, and nothing is too much for him to handle. I know God had his hand on us as we were thinking of names. This morning reassured me that he is ALWAYS in control.

Decisions Decisions

After scheduling multiple appointments, setting consults with Pediatric Surgeons, and getting lost along the way, we have finally made a decision to go with Texas Children's Hospital downtown.

We were first referred to Memorial Hermann Hospital where we met some incredible people. We not only felt like family there, but were shown that we were a priority and not just another number. Kudos to UT Physicians and all that they did to make us feel welcomed and loved. Jennifer, the genetics counselor, was so helpful. I cannot say enough good things about our short experience there. We knew it was going to be a hard choice between the two hospitals, but it was more difficult than we had expected. My phone call to let Jennifer know of our decision put my fears to rest. She openly informed me that she too had a daughter who required intensive care, and she had gone to Texas Children's. She respected our choice and wished us the best of luck. I was grateful for both her candid remarks and genuine care.

Our experience with Texas Children's was much the same as our Memorial visit. We felt comforted by the staff and were impressed by the in-depth discussion of Brooklyn's diagnosis. What ultimately sold us was the NICU. If any of you has ever had to be in intensive care, you would appreciate the heck out of this place. There are one to two nurses assigned to each baby. The lighting, sound, and overall ambiance is centered on providing an optimal environment for recovering children. We were immediately drawn to the compassion each person had in wanting the best for each child.

We are now in the process of getting my records transferred to Texas Children's. Once they obtain copies of everything, a follow-up consultation will be scheduled and a high-risk obstetrician will be assigned to me. We will get to meet the entire staff who may be working with Brooklyn and I throughout the process. I'm overall very pleased with our decision. Even though it was one of the toughest I've had to make, I feel confident Brooklyn will get the best care. Either hospital would have done an excellent job, but Texas Children's sets the bar just a little bit higher than the rest. 16 weeks to go! I've been so blessed to have an easy ride on the pregnant train, and I hope that the remaining weeks prove to be the same.

Even though we've got a long road ahead, I look forward to seeing how God moves in each step. He has already done so much to show that he is here.

We love you Brooklyn.

One year

This weekend my husband and I celebrated our one year anniversary. I can honestly say these past 12 months have been so wonderful. I can't believe it's already October again. It seems like last week we were cutting the cake and setting flight to Barcelona. So much has happened this year it's unbelievable. With Brooklyn on the way, I can only feel like our life has stepped into fast forward. I am reminded each day of how quick life can move. I want to make sure and take in every second. Look at the little moments and cherish them. I've only been given this one life and I want to make sure I live it with passion. I want to laugh at my mistakes, learn from my failures, and love with all I have. I'm so thankful for what I've been given and I want to take nothing for granted.

Last night we actually went out on a date. It's been forever since we put on something more than jeans and tees and attempted to look presentable. It was nice to go out and reminisce on our favorite moments from this year. We both agreed that finding out about Brooklyn pretty much topped them all. I can remember waking up that morning, realizing Mother Nature was a week late. In a semi-panic I took the test to see that little plus sign appear on the screen. I was so nervous to tell Jered. Before I could even get in the shower I ran upstairs and jumped on the bed where he was still sleeping. I whispered, "I think I'm pregnant", and immediately his eyes shot open. You see, we hadn't really been planning on having children this soon. It just sort of happened. But after the shock and awe faded, we began to share a mutual excitement for our new addition.

I love that moment and will never forget it. I consider myself blessed to have a husband who loves me so much. Sure we have our daily struggles, but overcoming them with him is the best reward. I'm ecstatic to see what's in store for us this next year. I have no doubts I will be amazed once more at God's willingness to bless us. We are grateful for everything and leave nothing to chance.

Company During Delivery

Today I had my 28 week ultrasound and glucose test with Dr. I. First of all, WOW. Can we discuss how sweet and disgusting that drink is? Do you remember those little plastic bottles that came in bulk and had the foil caps? I can't remember their name, but my Grams used to give them to us as kids. It's like a flat, super sweet, stale Kool-Aid. I had the pleasure of trying the "orange" flavor which is now making Brooklyn go absolutely nuts.

The ultrasound went well. Brooklyn currently weighs 2.8 pounds and is in the 15th percentile. This may sound low, but it's expected for CDH babies. Because their abdomens measure smaller, they tend to be on the petite side. Her heart rate is 135, and lung to head ratio is currently 1.25. The LHR is a bit lower this time around but still within the, "let's not panic yet" range. They won't begin to worry too much unless it hits below 1. Her kidney, stomach, and liver still seem to be down below the diaphragm. However, the doctor did suspect the tip if the liver may be creeping up in the chest cavity. It's not enough for them to worry at this point and we'll know more once I take my second MRI in 4 weeks. I'll come back in 2 weeks for a regular ultrasound and follow-up with Dr. I. My appointments from here on out will be more frequent to monitor growth and development.

The good news is she's growing well! We finally got a decent 3D image of her this time. For the past several attempts she's had her hand over her face. Stubborn little Hales! The technician had to shake her a little today to get a good view. It was quite entertaining watching her pout her dainty lips. I guess we were interrupting her nap time.

I also found out that my best friend Madeline will be able to stay in the delivery room at birth. She's in her third year of medical school and will hopefully get a lot of experience from it. I'm so excited she'll be there for that moment, and I know Jered will be just as thrilled. He hasn't been too tickled about that leg of the journey. Hopefully having Maddie in the room will ease his nerves a bit.

All in all it was a good check up. We can only stay positive and hope for the best. We know God is watching over our little angel. We will continue to pray for her strength and will to fight. We love you precious Brooklyn and can't wait to meet you.

Never Again

After my ultrasound yesterday, I had a dentist appointment to fill some cavities .... 3 to be exact. Note to self; if ever again you find yourself pregnant with cavities, WAIT until after the baby is born to have them filled. Why you may ask? Because the amazing drug "epinephrine" used to numb your mouth cannot be used on expectant mothers. Instead, they give you this weak sauce of a concoction that lasts approximately five minutes.

No one really cares for the dentist, but it's a necessary evil we must all face. Nonetheless, I'm strongly debating on ever stepping foot inside one after yesterday's shenanigans. I felt every drill, every poke, every pry, and every additional shot. Yes that's right, additional shots because the numbing drug doesn't last long enough for the dentist to reach over, grab a utensil, and begin work. It was awful. The dentist kept saying how well I was doing and all I kept thinking was, "be quiet and hurry up". All three cavities were filled, all on separate sides of my mouth. This means that by the time he would finish with one, the next had complete feeling back (sans numbness). The final straw was towards the end when the dental assistant decided to put these metal wedges in between my teeth to separate them. I had never before had this done, and why on Earth they would choose this day to start I have no idea. These metal plates were pushed between my teeth and then cranked open with a metal utensil. "Wedges" were placed in the gaps to keep my teeth separated. My eyes began to water as I tried to endure the pain, repeating to myself that it would all be over shortly.

The whole experience still gives me the heebie-jeebies. I can only give advice to all current pregnant women to hold off on dental work. For the LOVE of all that is holy, HOLD OFF!

The day just got weird after that. I drove home, realized I'd left my wedding ring in the lobby of the dentist office, had to get Jered's Mom to bring it home, my dog got mauled by the neighbor's dog, and the cops were called on us for "disturbing the peace". Apparently listening to music in your parked car outside your house is not wise. At 8:30 pm the neighbors called the police on us because the bass was too loud. I think the cop realized after catching a glimpse of my huge belly that we weren't a couple of thugs rebelling against our parents.

Let's just say it was a crazy end to a crazy day. I'm glad it's finally over and I can get back to the monotony sitting on my work desk.

While I Wait, I Will Nest

I thought nausea was supposed to be a first trimester thing.

I'll admit that I've been really lucky to have had an easy pregnancy up until this point, but recently I've been sick to my stomach, very sore, and feeling faint. It seems like after lunch and each night before bed I feel my worst. If this is a sign of what the next 8 weeks will bring, then I'm not looking forward to them.

I had a check-up yesterday with Dr. I. He weighed me, took my blood pressure, and checked Brooklyn's heart rate. Everything went well and her heartbeat is still strong. Next week I go back for a growth and development ultrasound. These are the important appointments because they help us get a grasp on how well her lungs are growing. I'm hoping for positive news. Our last ultrasound showed that her lung-to-head ratio went down which scares me a little. Even though they say it's not time to panic, every little decrease worries me. November 1st will be our meeting with the pediatric surgeon. They will take another MRI of Brooklyn as well as an echocardiograph to check her heart structure and function. This will be the last crucial set of tests that help determine her prognosis when born. It will also help us be better prepared on the obstacles we will face. Jered and I keep our spirits up and have faith she will be a strong girl. It's difficult knowing the hardest part is yet to come, but we prepare daily by praying and giving praise to God. It is ultimately in his hands.

As for now, I have begun the nesting phase. I've finally started getting serious about the nursery. My husband LOVES every little project I bring home for him to assemble. My shower last weekend went better than expected and I can't wait for the next one in about three weeks. Brooklyn's room is already starting to fill up and it's becoming quite real that we will have a child soon. The closer December 16th gets, the more nervous, excited, and preoccupied I become. I cannot wait for our precious little girl to be here. Her presence is greatly anticipated by so many friends and family.

Hurry up Brooklyn; you know your parents are impatient!

7 Weeks

Only 7 weeks until our girl arrives. We are thrilled, anxious, and running around like mad men. This past week has been insane. I came in last Monday to find out that my attorney put her resignation in and is leaving the firm. Three days later I get a call from Human Resources saying they are going to have to let me go. WHAAAA?? I'm 8 months pregnant AND unemployed? Perfect.

Actually it is working out as a blessing in disguise. Originally, I wasn't going to be paid for my maternity leave and would have come back quick for that paycheck. My firm has been gracious enough to offer me four months' severance and insurance coverage until the end of the year. Mini vacay here I come! Well kind of. I'm at least thankful that I will be able to spend maximum time at the hospital while Brooklyn is in the NICU. It would have been impossible to come back to work with her there. This way, I can be there day and night making sure my little girl is getting the best care possible. The job hunt will begin shortly after the New Year. I'm hopeful that God has the perfect plan in store for me and my family. I'm actually a bit excited to see what he's come up with.

This week also begins our twice a week biophysical scans. Yes, twice a week I'll go to have an ultrasound done to monitor Brooklyn's heart, growth and development. Our appointment on Tuesday brought some decent news. It seems as if her liver is still down and her LHR has improved. She currently weighs 3.7 pounds which, as always, is a little on the petite side. They assured us though that she is still within the normal range and there should be nothing to worry about as far as her size is concerned.

These next few weeks are going to be packed. We've got showers, birthdays, Thanksgiving, and Christmas quickly approaching. The holidays are always a rush, but this year seems a bit more intense. We will take our days in stride and be thankful for the life we've been given. God has been amazing so far, and I know he still has some tricks up his sleeves. I'm itching with anticipation but reminded daily of the patience I'm going to need in the months ahead.

Here's to four months pay and no work! Woo Hoo!

2 Day Madness

I can't believe it's November already! Time is flying by. The past two days have been filled with a total of seven doctor's appointments. Let's just say I'm glad to be back at work. Starting it all off Monday morning was our Echocardiograph on Brooklyn. This is the ultrasound that focuses mainly on her hearts function and structure. Everything looks about the same as our first one done at 23 weeks. The heartbeat is still strong, the blood flow is still good, and there doesn't seem to be anything of major concern. They did see some backflow in one of the valves, but they said it's not enough to worry at this point. This was our last Echo until she arrives.

After our heart evaluation, we grabbed a bite to eat then headed to my ultrasound and MRI appointments. In the ultrasound, they estimated her weight as being 4.1 pounds. Go Brooklyn! She is still of course on the small side, but well on her way to being a healthy weight at birth. During the ultrasound she would open and close her mouth like she was talking to us. It was too cute. They finished the measurements and reported that her growth is on schedule and everything looked favorable.

On to the MRI … ….. UGH. I hate this machine. They strap you down on this hard board and insert you into a hole that's smaller than a hula hoop. They have to put this magnetic board over your stomach which puts pressure on your body. Because I'm pregnant, they had to roll up towels and make a "box-like" structure to have it sit up higher. This just caused me to sweat the whole time. The promised thirty minutes turned into an hour because Brooklyn kept moving around. I take it she was about as comfortable as I was and wanting to get out of there. The good news is they got the images they needed and overall everything looks about the same as my last scan. The liver and stomach are still down, and only bowel is seen in her chest cavity. It did look like the kidney was creeping up in the back, but they didn't seem too concerned about this. Their main focus is the liver.

As long as this organ stays down, Brooklyn's prognosis remains encouraging.

Our meeting with Dr. O went well also. He reviewed her MRI pictures from both the first scan and most recent one. He seemed upbeat, but reinforced that we will not know anything for certain until she is born. Not knowing the future is the hardest part. No matter how favorable her outcome may look in-utero, things can change very quickly once she is born.

Yesterday went much the same, this time I was without my crew. Jered had to return to work, as did my Mom and Dad. Flying solo, I got to take another tour of the NICU and Ronald McDonald house. I got more information this time and was really impressed with my Nurse Coordinator Bella. From beginning to end she went through the process of our arrival up to our departure. It was good to get familiar with the different sets of hallways and elevators so we can be somewhat prepared in the maze.

After my tour, I met with the Neonatologist. This is the team of doctors that will monitor Brooklyn before and after surgery. He was by far the most realistic and rational one I had spoken with. He wanted to make sure that I could expect the worst but hope for the best. He again made it known that this condition is solely based on how well Brooklyn does after birth, and if her lungs are able to sustain her. He went over the process of them taking Brooklyn right after delivery and made certain that I start preparing for that moment. It's going to be hard watching them take her from me before I can even hold her, but I know it's what will be best. They will immediately put a tube down her throat to support breathing and monitor her vitals. She will be wheeled away with Jered to the warming station and then to the NICU. No matter how much I prepare, I know this will be hard. I just have to stay positive and know that God will be with her at all times.

My last appointment was a standard biophysical scan or ultrasound. Everything went as planned and all looked well with her muscle tone and movement. This is the test I will go in twice a week for. I'm sure to be sick of ultrasounds by the time she gets here. All in all it was a busy two days. I'm glad to be able to sit back and take it all in. This next month is sure to move quickly, and I cannot wait to see my little girl. Thank you for all the prayers and support for Brooklyn. They are working and God has been faithful. Keep em' coming.

Guinea Pig

It's always both exciting and intimidating to be the guinea pig. The "rush" feeling of being the first is exhilarating, but not knowing the outcome can be nerve-racking. That is exactly the type of feeling I got this morning at our appointment.

We went in for the usual biophysical, but there was an additional agenda waiting for us. A doctor who was beginning a study on CDH babies happened to be in the office and wanted to know if Brooklyn and I were interested in a trial study. Because there was no risk involved, I gladly accepted the offer to be his first patient. The study is based on oxygen and it's affects on Brooklyn. First, blood flow measurements were taken via ultrasound in the brain, aorta, and vessels leading to the lungs. After this initial data was collected, I (the mother) was put on oxygen for ten minutes. They are testing to see if the pure oxygen has an effect on blood flow and oxygen levels in the specified areas. After the ten minutes was up, they took the same measurements again. Then, after fifteen minutes of being off oxygen, additional measurements were taken to see if any decrease had occurred. It was interesting to watch the doctor perform his test for the first time. I could tell he was hoping for the best.

After all the data was collected, he thanked me and told me he was excited to examine the findings. I will probably not know the results from his research, but being a part of "history in the making" was rather neat. It's awesome to know that advances in medicine are being sought out every day. That people, doctors, strive to find answers to the unsolvable. Being a part of this study only confirmed my reassurance that we are in the right place. Texas Children's and the Baylor College of Medicine is doing their very best to make sure we get top care.

I want to give a big shout out to the all who work in the medical field and for those on their way to becoming doctors. You are some of the most talented and hard working people I've met.

I feel blessed to personally know a few who will no doubt make a significant contribution to the efforts already in process. Thank you for having a passion to help those in need. Without you, who knows where we'd be.

Happy Feet

Everyday should begin with a pedicure.

This morning after my bi-weekly ultrasound, I decided to get my toes did before going into work. Best decision of the day so far. For the past six months, my feet have been neglected. After a certain point in pregnancy, you can neither see nor bend down to touch your feet. Hence the abandonment. You would think that this would cause frequent visits to the nail salon. However, my right big toe has some major issues. I don't even like wearing open-toed shoes anymore because of its unsightly appearance. Let's just say, "Houston, we have a problem". For one, the nail is in-grown. I would fix this problem, but the foot doctor says, "no go when preggo". The X-rays involved, plus the numbing shots, don't fare well for women with child. Unfortunately, this isn't the only issue. Evidently some bacterial infection has taken over my nail bed. Sorry if this is too much information and detrimental to the weak stomached.

Basically I'm embarrassed to let a nail technician touch my feet..... there, I said it. Even though I'm pretty sure she's seen a lot worse, I never want to be the topic of their conversation when you have no idea what they are saying. It's awkward enough when you can't understand their English and you end up saying yes or no to "How much longer 'til baby come?" I can always decipher the "pick a color" and "you so small", but let's face it, most of the time I'm wishing I had a translator with me.

I finally let down my pride and went in. I found myself apologizing every five minutes for my hideous toe. All the while the lady would nod and smile in my direction. I have a fairly decent idea that she had no clue what I was saying and was probably thinking, "This girl toe look nasty". Oh well. At least I have clean and pretty toes now!

Here's to Friday and happy feet.

Dear Brooklyn

To make sure you don't miss out on all the fun, I've decided to list a few things you missed whilst in my womb.

1. Can't breathe, can't sleep, can't walk. Because you (my child) are running out of room and currently smashed against my diaphragm, breathing and sleeping have become impossible. Not to mention I've adopted a nice "waddle" to my swagger.

2. Snoring. This attractive habit has become a unique attribute to my sleeping pattern. My growing mid-section has caused me to sound like a passed out, 300 pound truck driver.

3. No more toes. I can't see my feet or touch my toes anymore, and shaving has become quite the obstacle ….. If you know what I mean.

4. Did I just throw up in my mouth? Nope, that's acid reflux. It may smell like vomit, and burn like Hades, but it's just another happy symptom of motherhood.

5. WHY DID THEY PUT PICKLES ON MY SANDWICH!!??!!! Sorry, that was just the hormones talking. Don't mind them, they come and go as they please.

6. Is the heater on? Even though the thermostat says 60 degrees, it feels like a sauna just south of the equator that caught on fire in the middle of July!

7. Kick punch punch. I'm about to kick punch punch you in the head child if you don't stop moving while I'm trying to sleep.

8. Fashionista Extraordinaire. Now that I've grown out of every piece of clothing I own, sweat pants and hoodies are now in style.

9.   Did I really just dream that? Apparently being pregnant means your dreams become insane. Good bye romantic comedies and realistic future interpretations. Hello ninja parrots and oompa loompa musicals.

Can't wait to meet you daughter of mine. Let's try and focus on a quick and easy exit, ok? Thanks.

Love, Mom

4 Pounds 14 Ounces

I'm currently 34 weeks and 5 days pregnant. At my scan this morning they did the normal biophysical profile, but also measured Brooklyn's growth. She now weighs 4 pounds 14 ounces. She's a small little thing, but I know she'll be a fighter. I was hoping to hit that 5 pound mark by this time, but I'm reassured to know that she is still within the acceptable weight range. 4 weeks until they induce labor. It's hard to believe that it's almost that time already. Everything still seems to be going as well as expected. Her liver and stomach remain down, and she's practicing breathing like crazy. The ultrasound gals are always amazed by how active she is.

We are still in the process of finding a place to live. We are leaning towards renting an apartment near the medical center while Brooklyn is in the hospital. This will give us the opportunity to be close during her stay. It also puts us closer to Jered's job. I recently received an email about another CDH baby I've been following. She is now 3 months old and at home. She is doing well but requires around the clock care and medication every few hours. Because of flu season and her situation, she is unable to attend daycare. They are suggesting even up to a year of in home care rather than a public daycare. This helps us better understand what we may be faced with once Brooklyn comes home. We've stayed extremely positive and have clung to the hope that she will be fine and ready for anything once she is home. We are realizing though that this may not be the case. Right now we will take it day by day. I'm always the one that is prepared and ready, but it's hard to prepare yourself for the unknown. While we wait, we will trust that God will open doors and provide what we need.

For now, we try and stay patient…. which is so stinking hard sometimes!

Our Own Little Thunder Stealer

Brooklyn Elizabeth... Welcome to the world sweetheart.

Our little rock star couldn't wait the three weeks she had left. Instead, she saw an opportunity to stand out and did just that. 4:30 am I woke up to a little "surprise". In a state of shock I ran to the bathroom yelling at Jered to get out of bed. About the fifth time he finally woke from his coma and began frantically running around as I shouted commands. We hadn't prepared for our girl's early arrival. No bag had been packed, no plan a, b, or even c. Heck, I didn't even have my doctors phone number plugged into my phone.

So there we were running around trying to get everything together. We almost forgot about Rowdy, Jered's friend who had come down to take him to the Texans game for his birthday. Yep, you heard right, Brooklyn decided to steal her father's thunder and come a day before his own birthday. Way to go girl! With Rowdy in the driver's seat, Jered riding shotgun, and me in the back, we sped through the heart of Needville and up 59 toward Houston. I felt like we were taking Jered to the ER because he was completely out of whack. I directed Rowdy to the hospital while my husband mumbled some nonsense and stared intently at the road ahead. We got there in record time and were immediately escorted to labor and delivery. As I put on the fashionable gown and got set up on the machines, the nurse informs me that my water has in fact broken, and I'm having contractions every two minutes.

Shocked by my lack of pain, I felt more than ready to bring on the labor.

Then it hit me like the hammer of Thor. Blinded by the stabbing pain, it takes everything in me not to punch anything in sight and cuss like a sailor. They always tell you how bad it hurts, but you can't fully grasp the torture until you've experienced it.

Almost instantly I agree with the nurse that now is the time for the big needle. ONE EXCRUCIATING HOUR LATER the anesthesiologist arrives. Of course he's a male .... What's the rush, right? At this point I begin cursing the entire male population. Sorry guys, it was just in that moment I promise.

Amen, hallelujah, praise to the heavens. Epidural stands for everlasting joy. Labor was a breeze after that and truly it felt much quicker than it lasted. In just a few short hours and couple of a pushes, our Brooklyn Elizabeth came into this world kicking and weighing 5 pounds 6 ounces. With a full head of hair, I got to hear my baby girl's sweet coo before they whisked her away. My heart was so joyful and so distraught at the same time. It took everything in me not to break down as they sped her away to the NICU. I'm so thankful my husband got to be her usher. I could not have done it without his bravery and my amazing friend Madeline staying behind with me as I was sewn up.

They kept me updated as I waited to be transferred to our overnight room. Brooklyn was amazing. She was trying to breathe on her own and took the tubes, IV's, and wires like a champ. She was alert, active and fighting every step of the way. Her heartbeat was strong and her eyes were open. She was perfect. A few hours later I got to see her. I had held it together so well up until that point. The feeling of overwhelming joy, amazement, anxiety, and fear stirred into one as I felt her little fingers. Brooklyn was and is still hooked up to a ventilator, stomach tube, and IV's. Cords are everywhere.

Our girl is currently doing very well. She has remained stable with a good heart rate. They attempted a PICC line today so that medication would be easier to give. Unfortunately, they were not successful and will try again tomorrow. She will have to stick with the IV's in both hands for now. These lines will be changed often because of her fragile veins. We believe her surgery will be in a few days, but until then, they will monitor her and make sure she is ready to handle such a tough procedure. She's been a fighter so far and I know she will amaze us all.

The Lord has been my strength through these past two days. I'm awestruck by his mercy and grace. He has blessed our lives with such loving friends and family. I couldn't have asked for a better support group. Thank you to everyone who held out through the night and to all our wonderful visitors. We have wanted for nothing and continue to be surprised at the generosity from all. We are so thankful for all the prayers. God has been faithful and we will continue to put all trust in Him. Brooklyn has a long road ahead, but we remain confident in God's ability to work miracles.

Brooklyn, what can I say sweet girl? You've captured our hearts with your beauty. And don't worry, Dad isn't too bummed that you had to one up him. Just between you and I, the 28th is way better than the 29th to have a birthday.

Love you girl!

What Little Girls Are Made Of

Day three has come to a close. As I try to wrap my mind around the flood of emotions, I'm brought to a place where no one can fully be prepared. Being discharged after giving birth should mean that we get to bring our baby home. You see it all the time in movies. Mom in the wheel chair holding a swaddled baby. Dad carting the luggage and gifts. Smiles and awes by passerbies.

But that picture perfect scene is far removed from our current reality.

We will drive home tonight empty handed. We will leave our baby girl in great hands, but they will not be ours. We will be strong. We will endure. But we will carry heavy hearts to sleep tonight.

Brooklyn had a long day, but boy was she a trooper. After several attempts at putting in her central line for medication access, they were finally successful. This means that she has a semi permanent line that the doctors will use to make sure she gets everything she needs. This also means that her surgery will most likely be this Thursday if everything goes according to plan.

For now she rests. She has been so strong up until now and will need even more strength for the days to come. You can already see her stubborn side come out when she's had enough of people messing with her. But she's our stubborn girl and we couldn't be more proud. We will return bright and early in the morning to see our sweet girl. Because we left so quickly, we need to regroup tonight and pack some supplies we will need for the next few days. Our poor dog is probably freaking out right now so we hope to get her settled and taken care of.

Brooklyn girl, I promise we will be back soon. Hang in there champ. You've got too many people counting on you to blow the doctors minds. Show them what little girls are made of. I hear it's something along the lines of dynamite and determination… Or maybe that's just in the Hales/Barfield genes.

Love you more than life my little firecracker.

Surgery Moved

Brooklyn's surgery has been moved to Monday. She's still doing well but they want to give her some more time to remain stable. She's still very sensitive to noise and touch, so they want to make sure she is strong and ready to handle the procedure. They have put her on nitrous oxide to help the vessels in her lungs bring more oxygen to them. She is still on regular oxygen and will most likely be kept on both of these machines for awhile after surgery. They have put her on Ativan to take the "edge" off. I don't blame the girl for getting mad when she gets a diaper change or they move her position while she's trying to catch some sleep. She's still stubborn even out of the womb and I can only hope her hard head serves well over the coming weeks.

She sleeps with one hand near her ear, another trait taken from her aunt Jennifer. Jered read some baseball news to her yesterday while she slept, so she should be well versed on Jeter's free agency status. While she rests, I too try and take it easy. It's so hard to do because I want to spend as much time as possible with her. However, I'm still very sore and weak from delivery. I'm hoping this goes away soon so I can get back to kicking butt and taking names. There's a lot to get done apart from her stay here and I want to make sure we stay on top of everything. I meet with my HR director today to sign my severance papers and fill out COBRA applications. The insurance situation is the most important at this point. We both are covered until the end of December and then we will need alternative coverage. Whether that's COBRA or Medicaid I'm not sure. I should be able to schedule an appointment with a social worker today or tomorrow to see what our options may be.

We've got a long road ahead but I have no doubts we can handle it. We've come this far and won't give up. I know I say this often, but thank you again for all the prayers. Praying is the BIGGEST thing anyone can do for us. Brooklyn's got a lot of fans out there rooting for a big win. I have a feeling she won't disappoint.

Foreign Object

So apparently since delivery was so hectic, and a lot was going on, the doctors failed to realize they left something behind.

I had been taking 600 mg of Motrin and 2 Vicodin every four hours without relief. I really thought I had a high tolerance for pain, but this was not the case at the moment. I understand giving birth is kind of a big deal and that you can't just jump up and do a cartwheel right away, but seriously, I couldn't even lie still without throbbing pain down below.

Last night had to be the worst of it. I woke in the middle of the night shaking uncontrollably. The pain was so intense it made it hard for me to sleep. I took some more Motrin and finally fell back to sleep for a few hours. The shower this morning helped a bit but I was beginning to wonder how long I'd be so uncomfortable. I couldn't figure it out.

A few hours later I got my answer. On one of many trips to the restroom, a "surprise" was found…. Gauze. Measuring at about the width of a silver dollar was a wad of gauze that had been left inside me after delivery. It's no wonder the Vicodin hadn't been working. I came to find out that this is a huge "no no" in the medical world. They are supposed to take count of everything that goes in and everything that comes out with any procedure. Because my delivery had been so chaotic, the doctors failed to make sure they had followed protocol.

Way to go fellas, way to go.

So now I sit in the doctor's office across the street and wait to find out what else they may have forgotten. Pull me out some cash while your down there doc, these visits aren't cheap.

Shunting

Brooklyn is officially five days old and still fighting strong. Surgery is scheduled for Monday as long as she behaves herself. I'm really pleased with waiting to have the surgery and feel that the doctors are making sure she can handle it. Dr. O will be performing the operation. In my opinion and several others, Texas Children's is lucky to have this incredible man on staff. I've heard stories from other medical personnel that he is absolutely the best. I feel very confident knowing Brooklyn will be in his hands.

Brooklyn had a decent rest last night. Yesterday she was having difficulties adjusting to all the medication changes and her vitals had been going from one extreme to the other. The word of these past few days has been "shunting". Basically this means that Brooklyn's vitals race back and forth, up and down without much consistency. The doctors are trying to find the right "cocktail" of medications to suit her individual needs. Every child is different and the same thing that worked on the last CDH newborn may not be what's right for the next. Everything they do to Brooklyn is trial and error until they find out what works best. This is one of the hardest things to watch. Some of the best advice I've been given so far is "to not ride the roller coaster with her". This is terribly difficult at times but I just have to trust that the doctors have her best interest at heart and want her to succeed as much as I do.

Right now, Brooklyn is doing so-so. We are hoping as the weekend approaches she will begin to fall more into a stable pace and be completely ready for the Monday procedure. I know this is leaving out a lot of tiny details but I want to keep everyone focused on the big picture. Sometimes we can get caught up in numbers and logistics that it fogs our perception of her progress. Optimism and positivity are what our baby girl needs right now. Lots of love and prayers are the best medicine for her. Thank you again to all our followers and prayer warriors out there. You are not forgotten and greatly appreciated.

Our biggest advantage is God's hand on her. There's no better touch than the one that heals.

Holding On

Today has been good. Overall, Brooklyn has kept her stats at acceptable levels and continues to show some stability. As I sit with her now, her heart rate stands at 134. Her blood pressure is a bit low but still above the threshold. Breathing is elevated slightly, but I'm told that as long as the other numbers look good, she can "huff and puff all she wants to". She's really swollen at the moment and it's giving her a double chin. I wish this was a result from her being fat and healthy.

We travel home again tonight to try and get some of our life in order. That, and the fact that we've been wearing the same clothes for three days. We are also going to try and get Bella situated. Luckily, our fantastic neighbor has pretty much adopted her and even has her sleeping inside. We are so thankful for all the support coming in from all around. Even the small things we don't think about are being taken care of.

The feeling of helplessness has hit me hard today. I know that the nurses and doctors have everything under control, but I wish there was some way I could help. It's difficult watching your child lay in a bed, surrounded by wires, motionless. The sedation has her looking more like a doll than a real person. I know it's for her own good, but I want more than anything to see her open her big eyes and smile. Patience is always the hardest part of any struggle. We don't like waiting, especially in today's age. Yet here we sit, waiting. I'm looking forward to Monday. The surgery means we are one step closer to recovery.

I know there will be more bumps in the road, but Brooklyn just got a new set of tires. And those hills ahead? Bring them on. Our girl's got four wheel drive.

Hero

We got to speak with the fellow surgeon on Brooklyn's case this morning. Oletoya's team is still planning to do surgery on Monday if she has a smooth weekend. We were asked to sign a release for surgery as the fellow briefly discussed some possible risks. There is the obvious risk for infection and loss of blood as in every operation, but there are also some that are dependent on her CDH. One that hadn't been brought to our attention until now is the possibility of her abdomen being too small to hold the bowels that are currently in her chest. Because her body isn't use to them being in the proper place, there is a chance that the belly didn't reach its full shape. If this is the case, they will leave the incision open to allow swelling to go down and give time for her abdomen to stretch. We of course hope that this will not be an issue and her little belly proves to have sufficient space for everything.

Today they changed out the machines which pump her medications. I hadn't experienced this yet and wished I would have missed it. When they change the machines, there is a span of about 15 minutes were her blood pressure rises above normal levels and her other vitals do jumping jacks. It made me nervous and emotional to hear all the machines sound their alarms. The nurse tried to console me by saying this would only last a few minutes. Even though I knew what she was saying, I couldn't help but be teary eyed.

I'm hoping Brooklyn can get some rest for the remainder of the weekend. We are trying to limit our visitations so that she can stay calm. It's hard to imagine that leaving her alone is for the best. I'm slightly comforted by the fact that she will not remember all of this. We will tell her stories and do our best to make her sound like a hero. I can't wait for the day when she brags to her friends about all that she endured at a young age.

If only super powers came in vending machines. I'd pay big bucks for invincibility.

One week

Today marks one week since Brooklyn made her debut in this world. She sure is being quite feisty on this small milestone. Her blood pressure has been consistently low and she is currently on 80% oxygen. They have maxed out the medication that helps these stats stay at normal levels. As you all know, surgery was tentatively scheduled for Monday afternoon. After monitoring her vitals today, the doctors believe it is best to wait. She is on the chart for Tuesday but as always, this is dependent on how she acts tomorrow. An ultrasound is scheduled for the morning to gauge her pulmonary hypertension and check the strength of her heart.

We are praying for her blood pressure tonight. This is a major factor in determining when surgery will take place. Only Brooklyn can tell us when she's ready. Her stubborn nature (thanks dad) has us waiting patiently. As much as I wish to switch places with her, I can't. I can't speed up time and I can't make it all better.

But I can pray.

I can pray that Jesus be with her and that blood pressure rises. I can pray that her heart beats strong and her lungs strengthen with each breath. I can pray that with each minute that passes she fights harder to stay stable. As long as I keep praying, I know that God is in control. He knows the perfect amount of time she needs to be ready for the operation.

Tomorrow is going to be a long day. Not only will we be waiting to hear the doctors evaluation, I'll be working hard on the financial aspect of all this. I'll be on the phone, discussing our situation and getting together all required documents. With some luck, I should be able to get a better grasp on our circumstance. It's so hard to focus on things like money when your child is fighting for her life. It seems like nothing else should matter except getting that little girl better. Unfortunately, half the battle is dealing with insurance companies and negotiating our options.

A good night's rest is in order tonight. Jered will return to work tomorrow and I will hold down the fort. And by fort I mean our designated corner of the waiting room. Just like the Central Perk couch on Friends, our life revolves around a couple of seats. All we are missing is Phoebe in the corner singing "Smelly Cat".

Sleep well baby girl. Let's have a peaceful night.

ECMO

My request for a peaceful night did not come for Brooklyn. Her blood pressure had been low all day and swelling around her head and abdomen began to worsen. We had hoped to snag a room at the Ronald McDonald House, but unfortunately we were bumped due to several babies having surgery scheduled. The ride home was emotional yet again, but I knew Brooklyn would be in good hands.

Sleep for us came around 11. At 12:30 we got a call from the hospital. It was the nurse manager calling to update us on Brooklyn's status. She was very unstable and her blood pressure just wouldn't rise. She informed us that if she didn't improve, they would consider ECMO.

ECMO…. The four letter acronym no CDH parent wants to encounter. This device is the same one used in open heart surgery. It's a bypass machine for both the heart and lungs. This technique is used as a last resort for babies with CDH. Because there are several risks involved, the doctors do everything in their power to stay away from ECMO.

The nurse said she would contact us if this became the case, but she insisted we come to the hospital because of Brooklyn's state. We fled the house in a state of panic, much like the day my water broke. I prayed the whole way, asking God to be with our girl.

Not soon after we arrived, the word came. Brooklyn would have to put on ECMO because she just wasn't showing progress. My heart sank. As the doctors ran about getting things in order I felt like I wasn't there. I felt like I was looking at someone else's life from some distant place.

I pray that no parent ever has to go through what we witnessed this morning. I will spare the details on how helpless she looked attached to the machine. This procedure is not a treatment. It is only to buy the doctor's time to figure out why Brooklyn is so sick. Her X-ray showed significant fluid in her chest and surrounding areas. This leads them to believe that she may have an infection. They put her on antibiotics for possible pneumonia, and will monitor her over the next several days. For now, surgery is put on hold. To our understanding, there are bigger problems to solve before they fix her diaphragm.

Please keep her in your prayers. She needs it now more than ever.

One Day at a Time

We are reminded daily that this process is one small step at a time. Her doctors and we have adopted the motto "one day at a time".

Apparently our little Brooklyn doesn't like following the rules very well. It seems that every time the doctors think they have a handle on her condition, something else happens. We've been told repeatedly that Brooklyn is unlike any CDH baby they have dealt with. We like to think so too. However, it would be nice to get some answers every now and then. The surgeon came in this afternoon and decided to put Brooklyn on some diuretics. They are hoping this will cause some of her swelling to go down so surgery can be scheduled.

Because Brooklyn cannot be moved while on ECMO, the retention and swelling increases. Hopefully these new medications will help her get rid of the extra fluid surrounding her lungs. If this method fails, they will have to put a tube in her chest to release the fluid. There is much more risk involved in the second option.

We continue to stay positive and trust in the Lord. Even though my faith has never been stronger, it is not easy seeing her like this. I want so badly to fix everything but can't.

I can't wait to hold her in my arms. Just to hear her cry will be the most wonderful sound. Please keep the prayers coming. We are just beginning this long road ahead. Again, thank you to all who have done so much to support her. We are in the process of creating a donation page where funds will be collected for her medical expenses.

Here is a picture of our sweet girl and the new "hardware". No one else could look so good in wires.

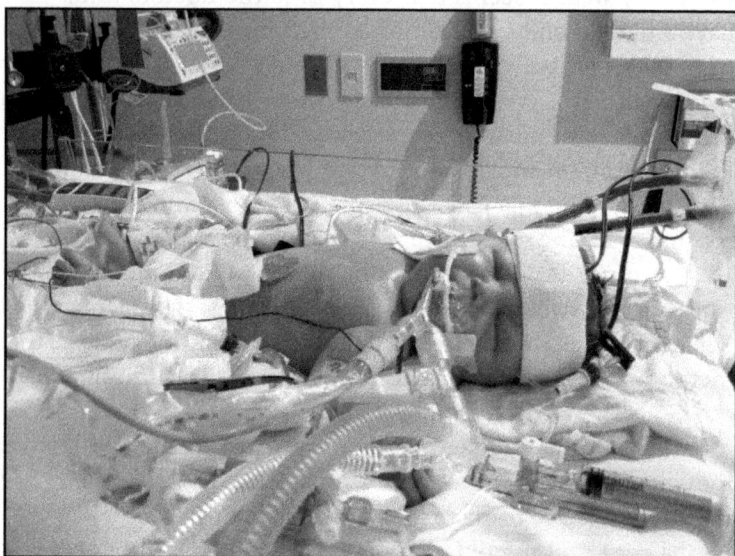

EEG

At 6 am this morning Brooklyn's blood pressure dropped and her heart rate spiked. She had been doing this occasionally but it would only last a second and return normal. Unfortunately, this last time it was sustained for more than a few minutes which had the doctors concerned that she could have had a seizure. There were no physical signs, but they ordered an EEG to check the function of her heart and to determine whether or not it was in fact a seizure. They are still running tests and nothing has been conclusive. Her vitals are currently suitable and she seems to be ok for now. They are also concerned about some bleeding coming from her umbilical cord. They are still trying to figure things out and wait while Brooklyn makes the next move. Her swelling persists but her urine output has increased slightly, which is good.

Miss Brooklyn is making sure she is getting the most attention in the NICU. She obviously doesn't want anyone to forget she is there. She has every doctor at her beckon call and is keeping them all on their toes. What can I say; it looks like we've created a princess who enjoys the spotlight. Ok little girl, that's enough. You've proven your point, now please start behaving. Your Mom is about to need an EEG herself.

Ronald McDonald

It's the beginning of day eleven here at Texas Children's. Yesterday's seizure scare has subsided as the results from the EEG come back negative. The doctors were unable to find anything suggesting she had one. Thank you Jesus. She held a fairly stable status the remainder of the day. Her urine output has increased and they are hoping to see the swelling go down if she keeps this up.

There is still no word on when surgery will take place. As the doctor explained last night, there is no set goal or status she must reach before determining a scheduled procedure. For now, they want to keep her as stable and "boring" as possible. Once they feel that she is not going to "flip a switch," and the swelling subsides considerably, then they will discuss a date for surgery.

They have increased a few of her medications to keep her as comfortable as possible. I have not yet been in to hear how her night went. As far as I'm concerned, no phone call means good news. The doctors will make their rounds at 9 am and I'll get an update on how she faired overnight.

Tonight we make the journey to the more permanent Ronald McDonald House off Holcombe. We should finally start to feel a little more at home and less like a couple if hobo's. The house at the hospital has been wonderful and the people are so amazing here, but each day we request a room not knowing if we'll get one until that evening. I'm so thankful for the many resources and people who care enough to help us through this time. I know I say this every post, but Thank You again for all the prayers. I will write another post this afternoon to let everyone know how rounds went.

One Day At A Time.

Letting Her Rest

If no news is good news than consider today a success. They have decided to leave Brooklyn alone to see if she can rest on her own without much intervention.

So far so good.

This morning they had to switch out both of her tubes going into her lungs and stomach because they were in the wrong location. Air was being pushed into her GI tract and they needed to fix this ASAP. Because she is still on ECMO, she technically doesn't need the tubes. The machine pumps blood and oxygen through her body so her lungs don't need to function. The doctors had to reinsert the tubes for when they try to wean her off ECMO. There is no word of when that will be. She has been on ECMO for 86 hours and counting. I'm hoping and praying that early next week they will go through with surgery. The doctors are still concerned with her pulmonary hypertension and the hearts ability to pump blood through her lungs.

Unfortunately it looks like I've caught a virus. After waking from my nap, I could not keep food down and have felt both achy and extremely weak. I'm taking no chances and am forbidding myself to visit her while in this condition. It's really tough not being able to see her, but I know it's best for now. She is already in a fragile state and I will not be the one to worsen her instability.

I will rest tonight and pray that this virus goes away quickly. Goodnight to all.

Where Two Or Three Are Gathered

No one has been able to enter the NICU today due to two surgeries taking place. However, I was able to get in contact with Brooklyn's nurse for an update. Early this morning the doctors rounded on her case. They have decided to decrease her blood pressure medication and slightly increase her morphine. They are trying to begin weaning her off some of the medication in hopes that she can be stable on her own. The nurse also mentioned that they attempted to lower her ventilation setting to see if Brooklyn could breathe some on her own. She did not tolerate the change well and so they put it back on the regular setting.

The surgeons came by to discuss a possible date for surgery. If Brooklyn does decent over the weekend, and tolerates the changes in her settings, then surgery will tentatively be set for Tuesday. Please pray that Brooklyn begins to show signs of improvement and that she is able to take the changes they will make.

Let's fill heaven with Brooklyn's name. Matthew 18:20 states "for where two or three come together in my name, there am I with them". Prayer is a precious gift we should not take for granted. Let us not underestimate its power.

This Is Her Show

Pulling up to the hospital this morning felt like coming home after a long vacation. In a weird way I felt "home sick" for the NICU. I had only spent one night away, but it felt much longer with the distance between Brooklyn and I. I was almost giddy washing my hands before making the trek to room C47.

Wow did she look good today. Her nurse Lily filled us in on how well Brooklyn had been doing. She is now completely off her blood pressure medication and still urinating at sufficient amounts. Her swelling continues to go down and her stats remain stable. Every now and then she'll get antsy and move around, causing her vitals to jump a bit. I think she's about had enough of this staying still thing. Sitting in the room gazing at the beauty we created had us at peace.

And then the greatest news we've heard all week came.

They want to do surgery tomorrow?!?

The doctors say that Brooklyn is stable enough for surgery. They want to take this window of opportunity to go ahead with the procedure. Since she has been on ECMO for 7 days, they feel it is time to proceed.

Dr. Y reminded us that prayers are crucial during the operation. The doctors may have science and experience on their side, but God is the ultimate physician. Prayer will be needed to guide the surgeons hand, keep Brooklyn strong, and ensure all steps are followed precisely.

God is already in this place. Brooklyn has touched the hearts of so many. She has proven time and again that this is her show and no one else's. Again she has ruined her Daddy's plans. Tomorrow we had intended to return to church, allowing Jered to play drums as therapy. I guess Brooklyn didn't approve of this agenda and decided she was ready for surgery.

We love you baby girl and your amazing timing. We wouldn't have it any other way. Thank you Jesus for a hard headed little girl.

God Is On Our Side

Brooklyn sure knows how to make a statement.

It wasn't 10 minutes after my last post that the doctors had a change of plans. With Brooklyn being stable, and most of the staff on hand, they decided that surgery would take place today. After catching my breath, and picking up my jaw from the floor, I slowly exhaled the word "OK". With no time to worry, and no time to think, we were rushed through the process of consent forms and protocols. Dr. O was in his perfect demeanor, asking me if I was ready. I responded with a simple "I trust you". His comeback, "Trust God".

We have been so blessed to be surrounded by such faith. I couldn't have asked for a better team of nurses, doctors, and surgeons. They are truly amazing. After being briefed by Dr. O, we whispered our love to our sweet girl. We promised her we'd be right outside, and that God would stay to hold her hand. We held her hand one last time, and then left her with hopeful hearts.

Waiting was anything but easy. Two hours passed without a word, and my stomach began to churn. Pacing, breathing, wondering, waiting. I couldn't get mind to shut off. The waiting room became smaller and smaller as more friends and family arrived to await the news.

One more hour passed. Just before I couldn't take one more minute, I heard the reception call our name. The charge nurse was on her way to update us. Standing patiently outside the door my heart raced; "please Lord let my girl be ok". The door opened and her face said it all. Our girl had fought hard and was doing well. She informed us that Brooklyn had remained stable throughout the procedure. Little blood was lost and she was doing just fine. A small patch was inserted to close the gap in her diaphragm. Everything was back where it belonged. Because her stomach is a little small, and her insides are a bit swollen, they will leave the incision open for a few days. Once her belly expands and the swelling subsides, they will seal her up and remove the vacuum.

Two chest tubes have been placed to extract extra fluid from her chest and abdomen. These will also come out in a couple of days.

She was a rock star. My girl had done it. She had amazed them all. One look at the new x-rays had the doctors in awe. "Magic" was the word used by one of the doctors and all I could think of was "Thanks be to God". He was there beside her through it all; our prayers did not go unanswered. A sigh of relief I'm able to feel as my sweet girl lay sedated on the table. Her color is good and she looks peaceful. She will rest tonight.

Tomorrow is a new day, and I'm sure it will be filled with challenges of its own. But for now, she will be still and at peace, recovering from her long and trying day.

Thank you to all who repeatedly prayed as the surgery was taking place. We are so grateful for the wide spread support Brooklyn is receiving. I know for a fact that this little girl has not only touched our hearts, but many more around the country. She is a true gift from God sent to show the power of his love.

Two Eyes and a Neck

My girl has two eyes today.

Well she's always had two, but for the past week her left eye has been swollen shut due to ECMO. The machine keeps her head tilted to the left and gravity has done its job on pulling fluid to that one side. For days we were only able to see her one little eye open. She also has a neck today. The swelling has gone down considerably and Miss Brooklyn is finally looking like the beauty she is.

The doctors seemed very pleased with her progress this morning. Today they will let her rest. Her perfect performance in surgery yesterday has won her some peace and quiet. They will reevaluate her tomorrow morning and begin the process of weaning her off certain medications. The tubes in her chest will stay there for now. Once they turn off the suction, they will have it on strictly gravity. After the fluid has ceased, then the tubes can come out. The vacuum on her abdomen at the incision site remains. Her belly is still not ready to fit all her intestines inside. Hopefully over the next few days they can remove this and sew her up.

She is doing great. We have finally hurdled the first obstacle and are on the road to recovery. We know there will be trials ahead, but we cling to our faith and hold on tight. Brooklyn girl, you've made it this far. Let's show the world how miracles work.

Have A Little Faith

It's hard to believe that a week ago today Brooklyn's stats had crashed to the point she had to be put on ECMO. She has come so far from those dark hours and I couldn't be more proud. Her perseverance is something to be envied. Even with all the tubes and wires, her strength surpasses my own. Where did this inspirational resilience come from? Surely I am not capable of creating such a masterpiece.

Of course I'm not.

This completely perfect angel could only come from one place and one person. To take credit for His work would be ludicrous. God made every inch of Brooklyn Elizabeth Hales. And for some unknown reason, He decided to give her to us. How we deserve such an honored gift I'll never understand. The word blessed doesn't carry enough magnitude for how much gratitude we feel. She has amazed us with her ability to bring groups of people together for one cause. She has shown us a love much greater than what we are use to. It's easy to get caught up in the mundane routine of life. This precious girl reminds us that it's not about us, but about how God moves through us.

Tomorrow we begin a new journey. Slowly but surely they will take her off the aids that are sustaining her vitals. She will need strength to hold her own. God has heard our prayers thus far, so let us not become stagnant now. Let us keep up the fight just as Brooklyn has shown us how. She will need our efforts. She's taught us to "have a little faith", and so let's return the favor.

Have a little faith my friends, and keep the prayers alive.

The Cadoodle Machine

I have officially mastered the art of sleepwalking.

I'm sure all new Moms can relate. We already feel like a dairy farm with around the clock feedings or pumping schedules. Then add on the constant worry about having a newborn and actually being accountable for a tiny human. Let's not mention you just pushed a watermelon from your body so you do all of this with a painful waddle. But even with all this, it's worth it. Just to see that sweet face you tell yourself you'd do it all over in a heartbeat.

Brooklyn is doing well this morning. I caught the tail end of rounds as they discussed the possibility of taking her off ECMO. Hallelujah!! The first attempt to lessen the flow on the machine will take place at 1 pm this afternoon. If she handles this well, they will continue to turn down the flow and increase her ventilation settings. By Wednesday, they hope to decanulate her from this dreaded Dr. Seuss machine. (It totally looks like a kid should be riding this thing down Mulberry Street, calling it a Cadoodle or something equivalent).

Her swelling continues to go down. She's looking much thinner which will hopefully lead to them removing the vacuum at the incision site. Morphine is keeping her heavily sedated, so even though her eyes are open, I'm pretty sure she's knocked out. As long as she isn't feeling pain I'm good. The poor girl has so many wires in her she's looking more like Clark Griswold's breaker box.

As one o'clock approaches, please pray that Brooklyn's lungs and heart are ready. Pray that her body is strong enough to take the shift in treatment. She's already proven she's in for the long haul; we'll have her back along the way.

All God's Children

So far so good. It's been quiet today in both visitations and Brooklyn news. She has remained stable on the current ECMO setting and seems to be taking the change like a champ. Later this evening, the doctors will asses her stats and decide whether or not to continue turning down the flow on the machine. They are cautious still about her pulmonary hypertension. With each adjustment to the setting, a risk of putting Brooklyn under stress increases. The staff is hopeful that she will sustain her current readings and be able to handle the tweaks.

I've been in and out of the NICU all day, continually asking God to be in that room. I ask him to keep her strong and let her feel the peace of his presence. It's actually been a good day for both of us. I was able to get some rest early in the afternoon and have enjoyed getting to know some of the parents in the waiting room. There is a couple here who just had a little boy. They have been waiting for the past three days to hear when their little guy's heart surgery will be. Every time they get a tentative date, another doctor decides to wait and they are stuck in limbo again. I know exactly how they feel. Sometimes the hardest part in all of this is waiting. It's bad enough to feel helpless for your sick child, but then having to sit and wait is torture.

Their family lives far away and they did not get a room at the hospital tonight. Please say a prayer for this family tonight when you think of us. Pray that they get a solid word for when his surgery will be. We are all in this together and I'm finding that not everyone has a support system like ours. I am so grateful for our family, friends, and for those who don't even know us but continually pray for Brooklyn. God has been so good to us, so tonight I want to bless this other family.

Thank you for helping me out with this request. May God be with all these little guys and their families tonight.

Never Lose Hope

Our sweet girl got a rude awakening this morning and has been working hard ever since. Mucus was plugging up her ventilation tube making it hard for air to get to her lungs. This is going to cause problems when they decide to turn off the ECMO flow. Brooklyn will need to work her own lungs in order to be decanulated from the machine. With the tubes clogged, this will be a difficult task.

Using a scope and suction, the doctors were able to clear out the obstruction. Because of the stress involved in this procedure, they plan on leaving her be today. Tomorrow they will pick up where they left off on turning down the ECMO flow. If everything goes smoothly, and her lungs cooperate, Brooklyn may be taken off the machine as early as tomorrow evening. As explained before, this device is pumping blood through Brooklyn's heart and lungs. Because of coagulation and possible clotting issues, the machine is recommended to only run a certain amount of time before the circuit must be replaced. It's about that time for Brooklyn's machine. They want to get Brooklyn off before they need to change circuits.

Another area of concern is the line going through her umbilical cord. This access for vital medications is pushing its life span. They are worried that infection is a risk because it has been there for so long. They will take some blood and urine cultures to check for bacteria. Brooklyn is on a low dose of antibiotics just in case. They need this line until she comes off ECMO. Please pray that there is no infection and that this entrance is available to continue giving her medication. An X-ray has been ordered to check on her lung. They need to make sure it has not collapsed because of the mucus block. We should get those results early this afternoon.

Our tough cookie is still putting up a fight. I am reminded each hour at how strong she truly is. Even with doctors swarming her, and nurses pulling on her, she continues to hang on. I thank God each minute for giving me such an awesome gift. I hope her story keeps reaching out to those who need it most. For those struggling to endure, look at Brooklyn and what she's overcome. If there's one thing our girl is teaching us all, it's to never give up and never lose hope.

Because That's What We Do

It's time to make a decision. The doctor's have been discussing different scenarios and options throughout the day. This much is true; the ECMO machine needs to be changed. Whether or not Brooklyn will be on the machine during this shift is unknown. As of this evening, they do not feel that she is strong enough to separate from the monstrosity. She is doing well, but they need her to do better.

There are a few options they are looking into. One is that they try and wean her as soon as possible and perhaps use an oscillator to ventilate her lungs. This is a device that uses high frequency puffs of air to fill her lungs. The doctors believe this may be necessary if they choose to decanulate her. The second option is to change out the circuit on the ECMO machine. This involves some higher risks which would like to be avoided.

Tonight they will let her rest in hopes that she will make a strong improvement by morning. Depending on her evaluation in the morning, they will determine their next steps. My faith remains strong in both the Lord and Brooklyn. With a team like these two there is no room for disappointment. Neither knows how to lose.

We must remember this is Jered's child. Failure is not an option. You former Hug It Out players can empathize. As a dedicated team member you are demanded to "suck it up" and "win, because that's what we do".

Baby girl I'm sorry to tell you this, but your daddy is a little competitive. So please do me a favor and up him one more time. Show the staff what you are made of girl. We are here to cheer you on.

Let's Do This

Ok Brooklyn, today is the day girl. The doctor's will come by your room at 1 pm and you need to be prepared. They will put some clamps on the ECMO machine and see if you can work hard on your own. Be strong baby girl. For those 15 minutes, be strong. God is with you so be sure to lean on him. I'll be there too, right outside the door. You can do it sweetheart; I know this to be true. You are a fighter. Show them how it's done. We love you so much and will be here when you conquer that machine. Breathe hard Brooklyn. Use those lungs like you did when you first arrived. Show us all how amazing you truly are.

Everyone will be praying for you. Trust me; the heavens will be filled with your name. Just a little longer now, it's almost time. You can do it girl, I know you can.

Just For Now

I have not lost faith. That is not what's happening. I remain steadfast in trusting that the Lord will see Brooklyn through. I will not allow myself to lose this faith.

I am allowed, however, to feel for my baby girl. I am allowed to cry for her and to be an emotional wreck at times. I can be strong. But right now is not one of those moments. I'll be tough in a minute. At this time, I just want to feel for Brooklyn. I know God hears a prayer in the midst of these tears. I have not forgotten who's in charge.

The first trial off lasted ten minutes before she fell. They need her to go a full 15 in order to prove herself fit. She had almost made it. The second trial didn't go so well. After about a minute she lost steam. They cranked the flow back up to 80 and let her level off. She is currently stable on ECMO. She's just taking her sweet time to come off. I know it is not my timing, but her and God's. She will let us know when it's time.

I just wish she would hurry up already.

I have not lost faith. That is not what's happening. Right now I just need to cry.

And The Oscar Goes To...

Today is a new day; a fresh start. One of the greatest gifts God gives us is the night. It allows us rest, so that we can start all over when the sun pops up. He gives us sleep so our bodies can recharge, allowing strength to build for another day here on Earth. God knows how rough a day can be down here; therefore, he gives us the dark so we can look forward to the light.

I'm looking more like the Stay Puft Marshmallow Man than anything else this morning. I guess crying your eyes out for several hours will do that to you. I'll have to admit it felt good letting go for that brief period. I needed the release. The only problem is that now I feel like I haven't slept in days…. and look like it too. Dr. O was so encouraging last night. He saw me when I was at my worst and came to take my hand. He reminded me to stay focused on God and to remember that he is still in charge. His strength is inspiring. I really don't know how doctors or nurses do this every day, but I am so thankful they do.

Brooklyn is full of surprises this morning. If one kid can make your heart do loop to loops, it's her. Apparently she has decided she is ready to be taken off ECMO. Early this morning the doctors did a trial off and she did amazing. She lasted the full 15 minutes and rocked the charts. Her gases and blood work were great. There is another surgery taking place next door to her, but as soon as that ends they will attempt decannulation. Another day in the waiting room is fine by me if it means our girl can come off this machine. They are doing an echocardiogram to make sure her heart is in tip top shape. She needs to be 100% ready for what is about to take place. Keep the prayers coming today. It may be a few hours before they proceed, but we will be fully prepared. God will know exactly what she needs come surgery time.

She sure knows how to put on a show. This girl will be fully prepared for her Oscar by age 2. Move over Meryl Streep, there's a new diva in town.

Legendary

Another long day of TV Land has come to a close here in the waiting room. Brooklyn had been one of three surgeries taking place in the NICU. Dr. C was the surgeon on staff today and took charge in removing the cannulas from Brooklyn's neck. We had an awesome nurse this afternoon that kept me updated via text messaging. She even took a picture of Brooklyn right before the procedure. She gave me a play by play as the surgeons and anesthesiologist prepped our sweet girl.

One hour later we got the news. Brooklyn was completely disconnected from the ECMO machine and holding her own. Amen! I know some of you don't understand the magnitude if this, but it is huge. From here on out, it's all Brooklyn. Apart from the ventilator, she will be on her own. Over the next week, the doctors will continue to turn down the rest of her support in hopes that she can use her lungs solely by herself.

In other legendary news..... I may get to hold her on Saturday! I've yet to have the privilege of feeling her weight in my arms. She still has both chest tubes in so I won't get my hopes up, but oh how I cannot wait until that day comes. Just to hear that it's a possibility means we are one step closer to her recovery. I'm so proud of our tough little champ. She has moved mountains today.

I can't wait until she is in high school and comes up with some lame excuse to why she can't do something. I'll just pull out these pictures and say, "you were able to handle this, so try again sister".

Take Your Time

I'm in love with a girl named Brooklyn. She's 18 inches long and 5 pounds. She's got her Aunts toes, her Momma's good looks, and her Daddy's hard head. She's sweet, stubborn, and loves to get a rise out of people. Her favorite game to play is freak the family out; she's a fan of practical jokes. She is strong and loves the Lord; she has touched the hearts of many. I'm in love with a girl named Brooklyn. She is my life, my soul, my daughter.

We knew there was a chance that Brooklyn might get worse before she got better once coming off ECMO. Little girl proved this to be the case. Last night her blood pressure dropped and her heart rate increased above the acceptable level. Now that ECMO is gone, she has to do a lot more work independently. It's a little confusing because although they need her to work, they don't want her trying to breath over the ventilator. There's a balance that needs to happen so she doesn't over exert herself. They have increased her medications to keep her blood pressure stable. She is also back on Ativan, the anti-anxiety drug. This morning they drew blood gases and were concerned on a few of the results. Because of this, they are doing a two hour blood transfusion.

Today she will get a new IV line, surgeon consult on her wound vacuum, replacement of the arterial line in her belly, x-ray, echocardiograph, and trial runs on weaning from the oscillator. They will discuss the possibility of putting chest tubes on gravity instead of suction, and discuss feeding. If this is what they call "letting her rest", I would hate to see what their vacations look like. Brooklyn is currently stable, but as we unfortunately know, this is a relative term. The doctors will monitor her throughout the day and make suggestions on altering drug intake.

We need a good day, one of rest and recuperation from ECMO. She's doing well so far, and we need her to keep it up. If the weekend goes well they will switch her to the other ventilator and proceed to lower its settings. It will be a slow process, but WE WILL see those tubes come out. We love you rock star Brooklyn. Take your time sweet girl, we aren't going anywhere.

Hope

Girlfriend got her hair did today. It's a good thing too. She was beginning to look like she needed those "smelly lines" cartoonists draw around their characters to signify stench. The goop is not completely eradicated, but we made some progress. She also got to change positions today. For a little over a week she has been stuck on her left side due to the ECMO cannulas. She is now situated on her back, allowing her left eye to not look so Popeye-esque. Regretfully, her head is cone-shaped. This is also due to lack of movement and bed positioning. It will eventually correct itself, but for now she's imitating the cone head clan.

Overall, Brooklyn had a good day. There were a few moments where her heart rate was high, but for the most part tolerable. Both chest tube have been taken off suction and put to water seal. Soon, they will be taken out. This is yet another step in the right direction for her recovery. The next big thing will be removing the surgery vacuum and closing up the incision site. The surgical team has already made a visit to assure the swelling has gone down enough for this to happen. They seem to be content with her progress and hope to sew her up within the next few days.

Slowly but surely we are purging hardware and throwing away wires. It's nice to see more skin rather than patches and stickers. Her battle wounds are present, but remind us of how far she has come. Soon enough those scars will fade, and she will be completely whole once more. A long lost friend of mine came to visit yesterday, and reminded me again of how God is moving through this tiny child. Brooklyn has shown us a deeper compassion for the Lord and his people. We are encouraged by her strength, and inspired by her will to endure. Even amongst the trials set before her, she is able to persevere. We have all learned this lesson before, but somehow it reaches deeper this time. It may have to do with her mountain being larger than normal, or her being smaller than average. We see how much she has gone through and our troubles seem to vanish. Our debt shrinks, and our unemployment fades to the background. These struggles seem minimal compared to her fight. No matter your battle in life right now, know that God has a plan. He sees where you are, and knows your pain. He will not let you carry the burden alone. If this fragile little girl can conquer these trials, I sure as heck can handle the bills. It puts things in perspective wouldn't you say?

Romans 5:3-5 "Not only so, but we also glory in our sufferings, because we know that suffering produces perseverance; perseverance, character; and character, hope. And hope does not put us to shame, because God's love has been poured out into our hearts through the Holy Spirit, who has been given to us."

Hope does not put us to shame. Thank you Brooklyn for letting us see the light.

All in Due Time

No excitement today means happy parents. Brooklyn had an uneventful and good rest last night. Today and tomorrow they will let her relax, and refrain from changing anything to her treatment regimen. She's looking better every day. After the weekend passes, the doctors will discuss taking her chest tubes out and sewing up her abdomen. Each tube that comes out means another step closer to holding her. They unfortunately got my hopes up a few days ago. I knew it was not in my best interest to hang onto the possibility, but I did. Even though it kills me, I will continue to be patient. The waiting will only make that moment more special.

Jered and I had gone home last night to try and attempt some damage control on our house. It literally looked and smelled like a dumpster. We were finally able to move some clutter around to see the carpet. We needed to get some type of organization going for the people coming to help us pack and move. This coming Wednesday our apartment becomes available. Although there is no rush, we told our current landlord we'd be out by the 1st. Most of our stuff will be crammed into a storage unit, and only a small amount will have the privilege of coming to the new place. We only signed a four month lease in hopes to find a permanent home. But the more I think about it, the more I feel we won't be ready to make that jump. Most of our time in limbo is dependent on Brooklyn. A bigger determination will be our financial status and my job situation. I know that the Lord has a perfect plan for us. That's why we have done so well at "going with the flow". But it's still hard not having a place to call home or being able to decorate a nursery.

All in due time I suppose. All in due time.

The Spark

We've all heard horror stories about Black Friday, the day after Thanksgiving where shoppers risk their lives for rock bottom prices. Picture for a minute a 60 inch LCD, the one with every spec a tech guru could want. The one that's usually marked for more than your monthly mortgage payment. But not on this day. No, today it is priced at a mere arm and leg, perfectly situated in your budget. The doors fly open at 3 am and mass chaos ensues. The stampede charges toward the electronic section as the weak are trampled by the strong. A scream in the distant resounds, and a chill shivers up your spine.

Now imagine that Brooklyn is the TV and the crazed consumers are her nurses.

Our girl has the medical staff fighting over who gets to care for her. We've had several nurses ask to "primary" for her. In order for a nurse to primary for a patient, he or she must sign a contract. This contract gives them priority over the patient of their choice. When their shift comes up, they will more than likely be assigned to that bed space. Brooklyn now has a primary for both the day and night shifts. It seems as if the, "I love B'klyn" fever has hit hard in the NICU.

Every mother thinks their child hung the moon, but I was seriously starting to wonder what supernatural powers our daughter had. Then it hit me. Our daughter is filled with something people are drawn to. She has that "spark" you hear others try and explain. It's that same feeling you get at church when your favorite worship song is played. It's the presence of the Holy Spirit, and our daughter has it. It doesn't matter where you come from or what you believe, you will be captivated without control. God's presence is something that cannot be denied, and it feels too good not to take advantage. It makes perfect sense why our girl has become the center of attention. She has been blessed to be touched by our Maker, and He has chosen to work through this tiny girl.

Brooklyn is continuing to show some progress. She had a stable night and was able to rest again. They need her to remain this way for a few more days. They had to put one of the chest tubes back on suction because the fluid was accumulating too much. We are hopeful it will subside and they can move toward pulling them out. The doctors seem optimistic about her recovery, but remind us daily that it is a day by day fight. Brooklyn has made big strides, but we need her to keep on trucking. Tomorrow begins a new week. Let's pray for more milestones to be conquered.

Transitions

I left the hospital last night pretty upset. Brooklyn was running a fever of 102, and was mad because of the new IV they had to put in. Whenever she gets upset she will make the "cry face". I absolutely hate this face. Because she still has tubes down her throat she is unable to cry. Yet you can tell by her facial expressions when she is uncomfortable or unhappy. The nurse seems to believe her temperature spiked because she was angry. I guess I'd get pretty hot too if people were poking me with needles all day. I hate to see her like this, so vulnerable and hurting. I can't wait for the wires to come off and the tubes to come out. I feel so fixated on this at times but I know there will be more obstacles to face when this happens. I forget that my girl has been on morphine and dopamine for three weeks straight. Once they begin turning down these medications, there is a strong chance for withdrawal.

This morning she was still running a slight temperature. They are not certain what is causing this and will explore some explanations over the next few hours. Brooklyn had a fairly quiet weekend and is showing signs of progress, but there are still a few kinks to work out. The surgeons came by to tell us her right chest tube can come out by the end of today. The left is still producing too much to be altered. They also informed us that her incision site could be closed as early as Wednesday. They are going to start turning down her vent settings and hope to switch her back on the conventional machine. It looks like our girl will have a busy week. She has rested well and now it's time to work again. We will pray for smooth transitions as Brooklyn handles the changes coming. I'm sure she'll put up a few fights, but she wouldn't be our child if she didn't.

Love you sweet girl.

Feisty

Note to self; do not look when surgeon is changing the vacuum dressing at the incision site.

When the nurse asked me if I wanted to take a peek at how they are keeping her open abdomen secure, I thought I could take it. I am, however, regretting my decision to view the procedure. Now granted, I didn't see her actual guts, but it was pretty darn close. They have a small patch inside the opening to keep everything compacted. But still, seeing her open belly like that sent the butterflies in my stomach into frenzy. I do not get queasy easily, but something about it being your child changes that.

The good news is her right chest tube was removed. This enabled the nurse to change Brooklyn's position. She had become quite feisty and they are hoping she becomes comforted with this repositioning. The left chest tube and wound vacuum will remain until further notice. They need her to come down on the ventilator and show a tad more stability. She's been extremely active today and they haven't gone down on medication. They think she is active because she's starting to feel a little better. I want them to be right, but Mother's instinct tells me she's just agitated and ready to get out of that bed.

They also tried to get her to take a pacifier today. She kept sticking out her tongue like she wanted to be fed. Even with tubes in her mouth they can fit a small gumdrop pacifier in. Brooklyn didn't much care for it and kept crinkling her nose. Maybe she'll get use to it. We would like her to take it so she can be prepared for feeding. Right now they are changing out the bedding. The chest tubes leaked fluid all the way down to the bottom of the bed. I'm thinking to myself that this may be the reason she's been so agitated. Who wants to lie in wet blankets all day? Now that her dressing has been changed and her bed isn't soiled, she can sleep well tonight. Poor baby girl. She's just got too much going on. If we could get more of this hardware off we'd be in a lot better condition.

Repeated once again; day by day.

Get Ready.....

Fingers crossed, hold your breath..... We may get to hold Brooklyn today!

They are switching her over to the conventional ventilator as I type. If she does well on this, and her blood gas is good, then this afternoon we may get the chance to hold her. Our nurse wants to take this opportunity before they close her incision site tomorrow. Brooklyn will need time to heal from the procedure and that will inevitably push back the opportunity to take her out of bed. I should know something around 1 pm. She will need to be on the regular ventilator for an hour before blood gases are drawn. Those labs will determine everything.

I'm too excited to update anymore! I'll post another one after rounds.

Yes, No, Maybe Later

The nurse said yes, but the doctor said no.

Unfortunately I won't get to hold Brooklyn. Until the chest tube comes out, and the surgery site is closed, I must wait. Dr. J came by to discuss what will take place over the next few days. Tomorrow they will attempt to close her incision site. The surgeons will not know if this is possible until they get in there to take a look at it. The worst thing they could do is close it before she is ready. If the skin is too tight, there is a great risk for it to rip open. The doctors would rather leave the vacuum on until it is completely capable of closing. We will know more tomorrow when they attempt the procedure. When the site is eventually closed, her right lung will be put to the test. The tight squeeze may cause some disruption in the lungs healing. We hope Brooklyn will be strong enough for this change. Her lung has shown significant progress and she continues to come down on the ventilator. The left chest tube will be the next to exit her body. They are envisioning a removal date of this Friday if surgery goes well tomorrow.

She has become more aware and agitated over the past couple days. This may be due to a few things. She could be becoming dependent on the morphine and other pain medications. She could also just be antsy to get out of the bed. In the meantime, they are giving her Ativan. This anti-anxiety drug helps take the edge off as I've stated before.

Once the final surgery has taken place, and she continues to show stability, the next challenge will be feeding. But before we jump onto that train, let's focus on the now. Brooklyn has had a good day. I may not get to hold her yet, but she is working her way out of that ECMO room.

I told my Mom that if it's taking her this long to graduate out onto the floor, let's hope she doesn't think 7 years of college is acceptable…..

Keep it up girl, you are doing great

Honored

The ants go marching one by one, hoorah, hoorah.

Yes it's moving day folks and the troops are in route. Boxes are being lifted, plates are being wrapped, and backs are being broken. Oh what a glorious day it is.

Leaving the hospital last night was like leaving Disney World. Brooklyn had such a fabulous day and everyone was smiling and cheerful. Promises of tubes coming out and wounds being healed swarmed around Brooklyn's bedside with harmonious melody. Her blood gases were terrific and she was coming down on the ventilator every hour.

Then real life hit ….. Moving. Ugh.

I think I despise this word more than any other. In the past two years I have moved exactly 5 times. That's an average of 2.5 a year. Pretty ridiculous, I know. With that being said, I'm really surprised that I still have people willing to help me do it all again. Apparently I have yet to exhaust my resources. This in itself is astonishing. Brooklyn may be helping this factor just a smidgen… She is in fact pretty darn cute, and one heck of a little superstar these days. Thank you my dear daughter for rounding up the battalion. You've made our lives so full and we are amazed at your ability to bring people together.

It's also a busy day at the hospital. The surgeon called last night to get consent for the wound vacuum closure. They will seal up her surgery site with or without an epidermis patch. If her skin is ample enough, and the opening is small enough, they will suture her right up. If not, they will use a small patch (similar to her diaphragm one) to close the gap. They will leave a couple drainage devices to pull excess fluid once the surgery is complete. These will stay for a few days and hopefully come out when the left chest tube comes out. This will be Brooklyn's (knock on wood) last and final surgery. There is a small risk in needing to redo the procedure when she's older, but the percentage is quite low. We know our baby girl will fully heal and recover from the work being done. God is still on her side, making sure every move the doctors make is the right one.

We are beyond thankful to our Lord and Savior. He has discretion over whom he blesses, and continually shows Brooklyn his mercy and grace. I cannot express how truly indebted I feel for His love. Time and again He continues to comfort my fears. He knows exactly what I need at the time I need it, and has yet to not hear our prayers. Thank you God for this amazing journey. I feel honored to serve such a loving Father.

A Call In The Night

Getting that call at 2 am when your child is in the hospital is never joyfully anticipated. Instead, your heart begins to race, and your palms sweat as you hurriedly answer in a shaky panic. Your heart sinks a little when you hear the doctor on the line say; "is this Brooklyn's Mother?"

Brooklyn took surgery yesterday fairly well. She lost little blood and was in stable condition after the procedure. However, her blood pressure remained low hours after the doctors sewed her up. They had to use an epidermis patch because her skin was too tight. She did not look like herself when we finally got the chance to see her. Very heavily sedated, she looked like she'd been put through the ringer. Added dopamine was given later to help with the pain she may feel once waking up.

Jered and I left our baby girl last night to come home to our new apartment. Brooklyn was in decent condition and we felt it best for her to rest without interruption. The call at 2 am was not expected.

The doctor was calling to inform me that Brooklyn was still running a high temperature of 102. Because this fever has been present for the past few days, they fear it may be an infection. Blood was drawn last night to be tested for everything imaginable. Since it is flu and viral season, they want to cover all their bases. I'm heading to the hospital shortly to find out what's going on with our girl. They have already begun antibiotics and Tylenol for pain. Please pray that whatever this is will go away fast. Pray that it is nothing serious and just a reaction from surgery. We know our girl is tough, but I would hate to see her fight an unnecessary battle.

Love you Brooklyn, Momma's on her way.

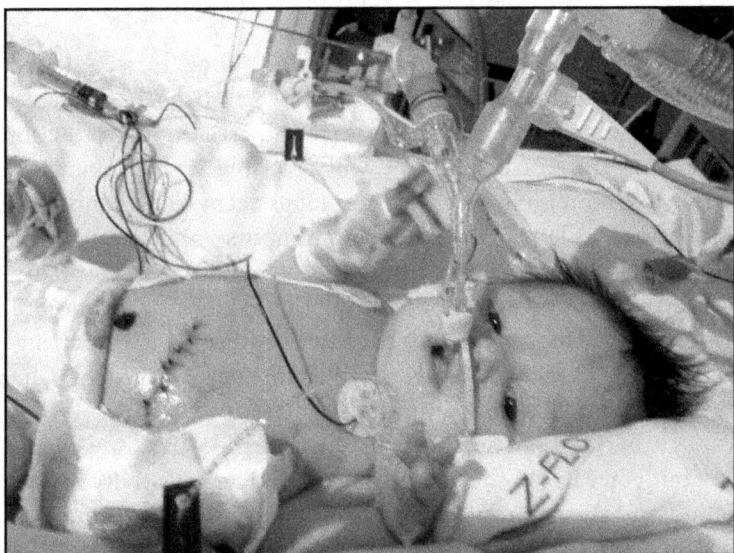

A "Feel Good" Christmas

It's another waiting game here at Brooklyn's bedside. During rounds today, the doctors discussed her current temperature changes and possible medication weans. Blood cultures were sent to be tested for infection, but results won't be here until early Saturday morning. All of the "rapid" ailment tests, like the flu, came back negative. As a precaution, she will remain on antibiotics until a full report is revealed.

They have turned down her Milrinone dosage (heart medication) in hopes to completely remove it at 6 pm. Her left chest tube was put to water seal but has since increased in production and flow. The nurse said they will probably stay on course to remove it nonetheless because her lungs seem to be handling it ok. Brooklyn's left cavity of her chest is now semi-empty after the surgery to remove the intestines. This being the case, her brain is sending messages to her body to fill the space with this fluid. It will take time for her body to become accustomed to this change in anatomy. Eventually her lung will fill the space. Until then, her body will work hard to compromise and adapt.

It hurts me to see her make that terrible face. She cannot cry but you can tell she wants to real bad. Her sensitivity has not let up, and she continues to show us her diva side. Just a moment ago her heart rate dropped and her blood pressure spiked. She was squirming and making the "cry face". I guess we were being too loud, because as soon as the nurse and I stopped talking her stats went back to normal. I swear this girl just loves the attention. Apparently we weren't giving her enough.

I'm hoping for a quiet night without phone calls. I don't think it's too much to ask for. Tomorrow is Christmas Eve and I want our girl to be well on her first big holiday. Everyone deserves a "feel good" Christmas, and I pray that Brooklyn gets just that.

Christmas Eve

Leaving Brooklyn to attempt a normal Christmas was anything but easy this morning. No one wants to leave their child behind to celebrate a holiday that focuses on family. It also didn't help that her eyes were open and her nose would crinkle to cry. I finally lost it when my husband wished her a Merry Christmas and told her we loved her. He told her to hang in there, keep fighting, and promised we'd be back soon.

She's still restless. It will take time for her to heal from this last surgery and it seems she's built a tolerance for the morphine. It's awful to see her in what seems like pain, but soon they will be taking away these medications. Her body will need to learn how to work without the added help. Nothing has been scheduled except for rest today. The only thing that made it easier for us to leave was a surgery taking place in the NICU. It will be closed to all visitors for the next three to four hours.

Christmas is just a little bit different this year. Even though our circumstance would appear grim, we feel as if this year has proved to be more than joyful. We were blessed with a daughter who has given us more fulfillment and love than we could imagine. We are forever indebted to our family, friends, and Brooklyn supporters. We could not have gone through this tough season without you. Thank you to all who have encouraged us and prayed for our daughter. Merry Christmas Eve!

Favorite Moment

I woke up this morning unsure if I was ready for big family gatherings. Leaving our girl, I felt more like the Grinch than Santa. I was far from being in the Christmas spirit and almost felt guilty for going to celebrate and mingle. Nevertheless, I grudgingly got in the car and headed down to Bay City, Texas.

As Buddy the Elf would say, my husband's family is "ginormous". They remind me of a combination between the Brady Bunch and the Clampets; one big peppy musical with a couple of rednecks tossed in the mix. Don't get me wrong, this is an awesome combination and I wouldn't trade them in for the world. On our way home my husband asked me what my favorite part of today was. After thinking for a few seconds, I decided that it was the moment his great aunt Bonnie put on this funky urban hat with braids.

Bonnie is in her late 60's and is mentally disabled. She may actually be the oldest living Down syndrome person, but she was never clinically diagnosed. Everything is an adventure to her and she gets so excited over anything that sparkles or goes on her head. This one particular hat was priceless. Picture a beanie with two braids and a pom pom on top. As soon as Bonnie set eyes on it she lit up. Placing it on her head, she couldn't stop laughing. She literally had tears in her eyes from the joy she felt. I wish I had just an ounce of her enthusiasm. She truly lights up the room with her love for life. She was talking to my husband about our new addition. She knew I had been pregnant and wanted to know where the baby was. After we told her she was in the hospital she asked what her name was. We told her it was Brooklyn. Her response was simply; "I know her"; and honestly, I believe her. Maybe it was the look in her eyes or the pause she took, but I truly believe God has placed Brooklyn on Bonnie's heart.

I needed the simplicity of today. I needed a dose of Bonnie's joy, and the love felt from surrounding family members. I needed the support from family and the feeling that they've got our backs. I needed the joy felt from silly songs and good food. I needed the love.

I can't wait to bring back some of this happiness to Brooklyn. It's been hard not being with her, but it will be good to return fresh and renewed. I am so thankful for a God fearing family who, without a doubt, is lifting our girl up.

Thank you Lord for a day filled with joy. It was much needed.

Brooklyn's 1st Christmas

Brooklyn is taking on her first Christmas like a warrior. As of yesterday, she is no longer on dopamine or antibiotics. Her blood pressure has remained stable and all blood cultures came back negative for infection. Her chest tube is still in place because they plan to start feeding her real milk. This is a big step and one I'm really excited about. Although she will be fed through a tube, it will be my milk. I will finally be helping in her recovery.

Well, we are off on the road again. Another day, another Christmas. Right before we left the hospital we got to see Brooklyn's eyes open. She had been completely knocked out all morning due to the morphine drip. She's becoming more aware with each day and I cannot describe the warmth my heart feels. With every blink and bat of those tiny lashes, my breath is taken away. She becomes more perfect in my eyes with every move she makes. Brooklyn is by far the greatest Christmas present I've ever received.

One of my best friend's parents came by to visit just before we left her. We were discussing the magnitude of a mother's love for her children, and how it's hard to believe God's love is bigger than that. Many Moms may even debate this statement. It's extremely hard for me to grasp that God loves Brooklyn more than I do. Yet it's true. God's love for us is bigger than our minds can comprehend. We are only human and therefore limited in certain abilities. When you think about it like that it's easier to understand, but that doesn't mean a Mother can fully accept the fact her love is surpassed.

I'm ok with the fact God may love Brooklyn even more than I do. He does in fact have a little more healing power. So yeah, I'm ok with Him taking over from time to time.

Why Not?

Dr. J called to let us know that her last day on Brooklyn's case will be Monday. With each new month comes a new round of doctors. Starting Tuesday, Brooklyn will be under new care. Dr. J wanted to fill us in on the schedule our girl will follow over the next few days. She promised to fully inform the new crew of Brooklyn's tendencies, or shall we say tantrums. Although it doesn't settle completely well with me that Brooklyn will be handed over to these new strangers, I am confident that Dr. J and the current nurses will advocate appropriately for our sweet little fighter.

Dr. J informed me that Brooklyn's heart rate has been dropping occasionally. This has happened before when she was on ECMO. Because her electrolyte levels are satisfactory, they are making sure it is not a sign of seizures. This process will help them determine whether these changes in heart rate are due to neurological abnormalities. Brooklyn does not show physical signs of this, but they want to be certain. Her right lung is still not progressing as well as the doctors would like. It is semi collapsed and the intermittent vibrations do not seem to be improving their expansion. A team is being sent in to suction the "goop" from inside the lung. This procedure is intended to help the function of the lung. It's hard enough Brooklyn is fighting with one functioning lung; but to have that lung collapsed is another challenge altogether.

She has been resting now for two solid days. It's now time for her to jump back into the ring. There is still work to be done and we must continue forward. Tonight they will begin feeding her milk in small doses through a tube. I am praying with everything in me that this goes well. CDH babies are known for their feeding issues and aversions. It would be awesome if Brooklyn could break this mold. She's proven to be unique in every other category, so hey, why not?

I've learned that it's almost impossible to not have high hopes for her. With her will power and God's grace, hope is anything but unrealistic.

Zero to Sixty

I finally made rounds this morning!

It's been a while since I have caught the doctor's discussion on Brooklyn's case. Now that she is doing better, they no longer begin with her. I use to know the exact time they would all gather outside her room. Now it's like trying to find Waldo in a candy cane factory, they are nowhere to be found. My luck changed this morning however when I rounded the corner in the NICU to find our Fellow Dr. T and the new Attending in discussion about Brooklyn. They have ordered an echo for this morning to check her pulmonary hypertension. The ENT team is also scheduled to scope her right lung. This procedure is done to gain a better perspective of why the lobe is susceptible to collapsing. During this time, they can also suction out any gunk or build up in the lung. Once they get this lung in good condition, Brooklyn will be a candidate for extubation.

I also overheard this morning that they are planning to kick her out of the Taj Mahal Suite she's been occupying. They believe she is almost ready to join the rest of the population out on the floor. Little Miss Princess is about to be booted from her castle. Everyone but Brooklyn is excited about this. I'm sure she'll throw a fit, but graduation to the floor means another step closer to checking out of this place.

The doctors will wait until she is scoped to determine if feeding will take place this afternoon. Fingers crossed everyone! They will start her off at 6 milliliters and go up from there depending on how well she takes it. I'm optimistic that today will be a good day. Brooklyn has rested over the holiday and now it's time to kick it in gear. She may not do zero to sixty in 3.5, but our girl is gaining momentum for coming home.

One Month Old

Happy one month birthday Brooklyn.

I cannot believe a month has gone by since you made your debut into this world.

So much has happened since then. The past four weeks have been a blur, but I guess the hospital atmosphere will do that. There is no concept of time around here. As parents, we cling to the "day by day" motto without recalling if it's a Wednesday or Saturday. You have come so far from that first week of life. I am amazed daily by your strength to tackle more obstacles. As I sit here and recall the past month, I am taken aback by all that you have accomplished. You have endured more physical calamities than I have in the 25 years I've been alive. Your efforts to take on such a heavy load would be enough to sustain your admirability. Yet that is just the beginning of your ability to catch attention. You have inspired hundreds of people with your story. God has been using you daily to spread His love, showing others that faith is a powerful tool. I'm so proud of you baby girl, and I'm sure you will continue touch all our hearts as you continue down this long road.

Love, Mom

Yesterday was a big day for our little hero. The top lobe of her right lung had been closed for a while. The doctors were trying to figure out what may be causing this, and tried several different methods to get it to expand. None had worked until last night. The ENT team had been called to push a scope down into Brooklyn's lung to take a look at the situation. They were only getting a better picture to determine their next move, but apparently they did more than that. Somehow while down there, they shook some things up. The lung popped open and began taking in air. A chest X-ray was called in and the results were obvious. Brooklyn's lung was now fully open. Looking at the comparison from the film taken a few days ago, everyone began rejoicing. Fist pumps were being thrown and smiles were flashing. This was great news. With this lung expanded, they can consider extubation and the removal of her left chest tube. Once these are removed, holding her becomes a very tangible option. I plan on getting to the hospital early to catch rounds again. I want to hear the discussion of what they have planned for our girl today. I am beside myself with anticipation of what's to come. We have crossed a big milestone, and I'm anxious to see what it may bring.

I cannot express my gratitude enough to the one holding this all together.

God, you rock my socks off.

She'll Let Us Know

I should have known better than to assume certain strides sought to take place today. I am here every day and know that what you hope for isn't always what takes place. I know these things, yet it's hard not to get excited about good news and progress.

Brooklyn's X-ray this morning showed some atelectis (lack of gas exchange) in the right lung. The top lobe is again collapsing. They have ordered chest compressions to try an open it up. She will keep the left chest tube until this lung starts working correctly or the surgeons decide it's time. The surgical team will stop by later this afternoon to debate the tubes removal. In the meantime, they will slowly wean her off the nitric oxide. They will also come down on her vent settings and begin feeding her today.

Brooklyn is still making progress, just with a few bumps along the path. She'll take one step forward, two steps back, and then four steps forward the next day. She wants to make sure we are paying close attention to every move she makes. For now, she will keep her master suite. Tomorrow is a new day with new possibilities, so I remain optimistic. As Dr. O would say; "she'll let us know when she's ready".

Million Dollar Baby

It always amazes me how exhausted I am at the end of each day. Work was a snap compared to this. It's not that my body is physically pushed or even exerting more than average force. There is no body building here. Rather, it's the amount of responsibility and decisiveness required for this circumstance.

Insurance was the root of all evil this time. Or wait, is that every time? Regardless, I struggled with automated voice systems and limitations regarding our financial status this afternoon. Without getting into the mucky detail, we find ourselves between a rock and a hard place. Basically put, we make too much money to qualify for certain resources, but make too little to pay premiums and put food on the table. Ok so it's not THAT bad yet, but the system is still frustrating. There are too many restrictions and guidelines to follow that, unless you fall perfectly into the criteria, you're up a creek (to put it nicely).

I know that it will all work out. Even if we end up paying a little each month for the rest of our lives, I know that God will find a way. He will not burden us with more than we can carry. I'm learning more each day how to let go and let God take over. There is no sense in worrying over the things I cannot control. He knows exactly what we are able to pay, and will not let us fall below our threshold. He will sustain us as long as we remain faithful to Him.

Brooklyn is worth more than any amount they throw our way. You cannot put a price tag on love; it's too great a gift. I am more than proud to say she will be our "million dollar baby…. in more ways than one.

Rough Start

Brooklyn was not happy when I walked in this morning. Her nurse had gone on break, and a nurse I had never seen before was trying to calm her down. She was doing all the wrong things. Granted, she doesn't know Brooklyn, but our poor girl was miserable. I asked how long she had been this way and the nurse responded ten minutes. Ten minutes? You mean you haven't called for backup yet? We are not dealing with a regular case here lady, so you need to get your head on straight. I finally asked if she had checked her diaper. It was no surprise that she hadn't. Brooklyn's diaper was the fullest I had ever seen it. No wonder the girl was throwing a fit. After the change, she calmed down considerably. About this time her nurse for the day walked up. She realized that it was time for Brooklyn's Ativan dose and that her chest tube was leaking again. She and I are beyond ready for this tube to come out. Unfortunately, there's been no time frame mentioned.

After the nurse changed the dressing around the tube, she suctioned out some gunk from the tubes in her mouth. Brooklyn's heart rate dropped and her breathing became erratic. The nurse said she had not liked the way Brooklyn's chest had been moving this morning. I agree, it looks like she is working too hard to try and fill her lungs. Our girl has mellowed, but she still seems uncomfortable. I hate not knowing if she is in pain. She's been flailing her arms about and making the cry face, but how do you know she's just not agitated? I think the nurses take a guess at this too. This morning my nurse said she looked in pain. She's called the doctor's to come take a look because Brooklyn just doesn't seem herself. The dose of Ativan has kicked in and for now she is asleep. Her breathing still bothers me however. Hopefully they will figure out what's going on.

It's frustrating because she will have an amazing day and then the next is total chaos. I'm about ready for a routine around here. I don't need any more surprises. It's all a part of the NICU experience I suppose. I can't wait to make like a fugitive and flee this joint.

Doh!

And the brain dead of the year award goes ... Lindsey!

For the next three days, Brooklyn is without insurance (insert gasp). You see, Brooklyn was suppose to come on December 16th and be covered under my insurance for thirty days. We both are covered under COBRA beginning January 1st, and so it was suppose to work out beautifully. (No gap in coverage). Well, since baby girl came early, as of yesterday she is no longer covered under my Humana plan ….. Way to go Mom. With everything else that's been going on, I completely forgot about this tiny detail. Unfortunately, my attempts to persuade the Humana representative to cover Brooklyn for three days have failed. Unless I opt for an individual plan, they will not cover us. The problem is I've already sent in the paperwork for COBRA to begin the first of the month.

These shenanigans I find myself in are becoming more and more humorous.

The next step is to capture a social worker tomorrow and basically tell them I am clueless. I'm thinking of just walking around the hospital with a sign taped to my chest that says "help".

I'm glad today is almost over. Brooklyn's had it rough as well. She has been very tense and the doctors seem to think it's pain. They gave her a bolus of medication for one hour in hopes to sedate her. So far it has worked and she is sleeping in peace. I'm praying that this chest tube comes out pronto. A lab was sent in this evening to test the fluid coming out of her chest. If the tests come back with certain results, the tube will be removed. The nurse thinks this contraption on her side is causing majority of her discomfort.

The only thing keeping a smile on my face is the breakfast plate I'm about to devour at 59 diner. You've got to love eggs and French toast for dinner!

Indy 500

Another day, another challenge.

Brooklyn's breathing patterns have not been acceptable in the eyes of her physicians. Over the past few days her respiratory rate has been fluctuating and they are debating the cause of this. It could be the plural effusion in her chest cavity or perhaps it is withdrawal symptoms from being on a high dose of morphine. An ultrasound has been ordered to get to the bottom of this conundrum. Meanwhile, her left chest tube remains. If in fact there is fluid accumulating on the right side, the other chest tube will need to be returned. I'm saddened to hear this is a possibility, but also know that if it will help her than by all means we will proceed.

Her feedings had seemed to be going well until this morning. Unfortunately, Brooklyn's body is not adapting to the large intake of fats my breast milk has. As of today, they will suspend giving her my breast milk and replace it with formula. The formula is less fatty and easier to digest. They are hoping this will affect the lymphatic system in a positive way. They continue to decrease her Nitric Oxide and hope to be completely off within the next few days. However, it looks like our girl will still be intubated for a while longer. The nurse has had to go up on her vent settings because of her sensitivity and agitation.

Another shot to my heart was the morphine situation. Brooklyn has been on a high dose for so long that weaning is seemingly difficult. The fellow informed us that because it will take so much time in between turning the dose down, she would possibly need to come home on morphine. It could be anywhere from 3-4 months before she is completely off.

Our sweet girl is still very sick. Her ability to fight is needed more than ever. You can tell she is growing weary from the battle, but I remind her daily of her strength. I cling to the fact that God has not left her and continues to heal her wounds. I must keep in mind that it is not my timing but His. He knows exactly how much our girl can take at each given crossroad. I find myself in moments of weakness where my patience wears thin and I get upset about the things I can't control. I know God is using this slow pace in Brooklyn's recovery to teach me about patience. It's always been a struggle of mine and He continues to remind me of this. There should be no rush in this process. If anything I should be grateful for the doctor's thoroughness. I need to print the words "one day at a time" in big bold letters above my bathroom sink. I say it enough, but lose its meaning on a day to day basis. This is not a race. I've been focusing on the other CDH babies' progress and it only gets me down. Brooklyn will get there when she is ready. I just have to keep fresh on my mind that God knows the perfect speed.

This isn't the Indy 500; although I wouldn't mind if it were.

Fresh Start

Brooklyn's right chest tube had to be put back in yesterday afternoon. I'm somewhat disappointed because technically this is a step back. However, our girl's lungs were so full of fluid that she truly needed the decompression. She was in such a better mood once the tube was put in place. A gush of liquid emerged as the doctor made the incision. Brooklyn is able to breathe easier now. They will continue her daily X-rays to monitor the buildup in her chest and determine the next window of opportunity to remove the tubes.

Her morphine level will stay the same. They do not want to chance pain since she just added another uncomfortable attachment to her body. She is still receiving Ativan as needed for comfort ability. I'm so proud of her. She is doing much better with her sensitivity level. She is able to handle more contact and sound which is very promising.

Her Nitric Oxide has also been turned down. It is currently set at 4. Once they are able to bring it down to 2 for a considerable amount of time, they will shut it off completely. Her ventilation settings remain fairly consistent at about 30 percent. I am told that even though she has chest tubes in, she can be extubated. This will not happen over the next couple of days, but we are getting much closer to that accomplishment.

Just another day here at TCH. Brooklyn will rest and hopefully take these changes with grace. Our Fellow, Dr. T, has left our rotation. This morning was bitter sweet in rounds. Although I am confident we have excellent new doctors caring for Brooklyn, I will miss the last team. They had become familiar, almost like family. I know they grew attached to her and will miss us as well, but the show must go on. Rotations do not stop in our presence. I'll just be glad when the holiday schedule is over and we can get back our regular nurses.

In other news, Jered returned to Needville this morning to collect the remainder of our things left at the rent house. It's been quite a struggle ever since we moved out. We had until the first of January (tomorrow) to be completely out of the house. The new renters were told they could move in after that. Apparently their real estate agent didn't abide by this rule and gave them the keys last week. To put it plainly, the couple moved into a house that clearly was still occupied with the past homeowners personal items. Who does that? The original homeowner was highly perturbed. It will be interesting to hear how today goes.

Tomorrow brings in the New Year. I am hopeful this fresh start will bring exciting accomplishments and new beginnings. Brooklyn, this is your year girl. 2011, don't let us down. We are counting on greatness from you.

Saddle Up

Enough is enough….. It is time.

I was going to wait until all chest tubes were removed, but I can't take it anymore. Nurse Michelle, our primary day nurse, has offered us to hold our sweet girl today. Nervous, yes, but I'm also excited to finally feel her warmth in my arms. I'm pretty sure I will cry my brains out, but I'm guessing that's acceptable in this situation. It will only be for a few moments, but I will cherish every single one. They may have to pry her from my gridlocked arms before it's all said and done.

She is doing fairly well today. They have put her right chest tube to water seal and lowered her morphine dose. It now stands at .07. Her oxygen is down to 23 percent and the nitric is at 4. All these numbers just mean that she is slowly making some headway.

Her feedings had been going so well up until late last night. She was being fed every three hours when at one particular dose she began to throw up. We knew this was inevitable. It seems as if every CDH baby has this issue. The doctors have changed her feeds to a continuous flow in hopes to suppress this reflux. Even with the spit up, she seems to be digesting the food she gets down. I'm still disappointed that she's not able to take my breast milk, but as long as she's eating I'm happy.

T-minus 30 minutes until we start the process of holding Brooklyn. It's going to be quite a chore to get her situated for the expedition. Itching with anticipation, we wait. 35 days has been entirely too long.

Saddle up Brooklyn, this is one ride you don't want to miss.

Time Stood Still

Day 35 did not disappoint. Everything about yesterday was well worth the wait. I couldn't have asked for a more precious moment than to hold my baby girl for the first time. My husband will wholeheartedly agree. Watching his expression as Brooklyn lay in his arms was priceless. For those few minutes in room C47, time stood still.

Brooklyn's first reaction was cracking me up. Her eyes wide open; she sat in a curious stare up at me. She had no clue what to think of this new experience. I couldn't have been more amazed by her tolerance during the process. For the past month, the majority of Miss Brooklyn's contact has been from a motionless bed. The nurse had cautioned us of the sensitivity babies have being held for the first time. After her explanation, I was sure our kid was going to freak out. I'm so thankful Brooklyn proved me wrong. In fact, once the shock subsided, my heart melted as she drifted to sleep in my arms. It felt like home to the both of us. Her level of comfort with me was the icing on the cake. I could have sat there forever.

Being held wasn't the only feat tackled by our champ. Yesterday also marked Brooklyn's graduation from the ECMO room. She has now joined the rest of her crib mates out on the floor. Goodbye luxury apartment, hello community dorm life. Despite a minor glitch in the ventilator, Brooklyn sailed through the transition with ease. She had quite the parade as she was wheeled down the hall to her new bed space. It's a little ironic that her middle name is Elizabeth, because she is not far from accomplishing queen status. Like royalty, she was escorted to her thrown by her faithful servants… or shall I say nurses. My husband and I are completely in over our heads. I just hope one of us will have the sense to tell her no when she asks for a pony on her 5th birthday.

I will never take for granted being able to hold my child. Even though these past weeks have been difficult, God has chosen to use the time wisely. He has shown me that life is not meant to be lived carelessly or without purpose. Every trial has meaning and every moment on this Earth has a lesson to be learned. More than ever, I've found the extreme value in compassion. I believe God uses each of us in different circumstances to unconditionally love and bless His children. Our family has experienced this firsthand. I'm so thankful God has tugged on so many hearts through Brooklyn. He is reminding me daily that it's never been about me or my situation, but about what He is doing through our struggle. With every second we spend with our girl we find ourselves in awe of God's grace. He has promised us all that He will never leave us nor forsake us, and Brooklyn's life is a constant reminder of this. Thank you again to all who have contributed in some way to her recovery. Whether it has been prayer, donation, gifts, or just love, we are forever grateful.

Queen Brooklyn Elizabeth thanks you as well. Happy New Year Everyone!

Answers Please

Can we rewind to yesterday please?

During rounds this morning the doctors decided to lower Brooklyn's morphine rate to .06. She has not taken this well. The drug Ativan, which is used to calm her down, is unfortunately not working as well as it has been. She has been getting a dose every six hours around the clock. Now, at two hours passed, she begins showing signs of discomfort. Her withdrawal symptoms are becoming more prominent with each change to the morphine, and it makes my stomach churn. With each grimace Brooklyn makes, my heart sinks. I can't stand to see her like this. We knew it was going to be rough once they began weaning the morphine. I have a feeling the next couple of weeks are going to be tense.

The nurse has called the doctor to check on her right chest tube. Her diminished breathing sounds and swelling makes us believe the tube is no longer working. With little output, this may mean our girl's chest is once again filling with fluid. It would also help explain her sensitivity this afternoon. You can tell she is uncomfortable even with the bolus of morphine they just gave her. Something has changed since yesterday that is causing her to dance in and out of stability.

Whether it's the decrease in morphine, chest tube malfunction, or another underlying anomaly, it needs to be fixed, and as soon as possible.

Big Migration

Our rock star is sleeping peacefully this morning thanks to her Ativan dose. The chest tube that was not producing any fluid is now flowing freely. The surgery team never came to check it last night due to the unchanged X-ray. They were unable to find any indication that her chest was filling with fluid, therefore, no examination needed to be had. It still made me leery of her obvious discomfort. But the nurses assured me there was no need to worry. Nothing has been changed to her routine today. The doctors have not come to round on her, so no decisions have been made.

She's sporting some trendy earmuffs this morning as a result of construction by her bedside. She was only moved two days ago, but it looks like she'll be in motion once more. The construction is expected to engulf the space around her bed. The charge nurse for today, and also our primary Michelle, came to deliver the news. She was about as excited as we were. It takes effort to move Brooklyn because of all her accessories. It's like trying to move Elizabeth Taylor and her jewelry collection. There is always a risk of extubation or shifting the chest tubes when moving her. I am promised that this next location will be her final destination. I know Michelle will choose wisely on Brooklyn's new space.

They are starting to round on baby girl Hales, so it looks like this will be short and sweet. I'll let you know how the big migration goes later today.

One More Time

On the road again....

During shift change tonight, Brooklyn will be transported to bed space C58. This will (fingers crossed) become her final home here in the NICU. Her current serenity will regrettably be interrupted by this excursion. I'm comforted by the fact that our primary will be around for the escapade. Little Miss Prissy will have her parade once again.

Swelling is still an ever present concern. During rounds this morning the doctors addressed the issue and asked that the nurse change Brooklyn's position more frequently to try and displace some of the fluid. They believe the excess edema is not a result of pleural effusion, but rather her leaky capillaries from being immobile. She still has both chest tubes to help alleviate the effusion, but the X-ray did not suggest a change in accumulation of fluid around her lungs.

Since the increase in feeds, Brooklyn has been spitting up. The nurse has said the issue is being watched and they will reevaluate the situation in the morning. Whether or not they will need to come back down on her formula intake is unknown. For now, they will monitor her closely for major fluctuations.

She is extremely stiff from her time on ECMO and battling edema. It's hard for her to change positions even though it's very necessary. With each shift, Brooklyn will let us know she is unhappy. "Don't mess with me", has become her mantra. However, day by day she becomes a little more tolerable. Everyone can see she is working real hard. I'm continually proud of her ability to be so strong amongst so many challenges.

My hero is my daughter, and her name is Brooklyn Hales.

Push Start

With the New Year comes new beginnings and a hope for change.

My husband and I were finally able to return to church this past Sunday. Jered is the drummer for the worship team and has missed being a part of Sunday service. Drumming is not only his passion, but a type of therapy for him. He has been itching for weeks to step on a stage. The waiting room armrests appreciate his return to his kit. They were growing weary from the constant beating. I was just as anxious to get back into praise and worship. There is something cleansing about singing to the one responsible for Brooklyn's healing process. The message didn't disappoint either. Following the pattern of New Year's resolutions, the theme of change was present. As a church family we were challenged to focus on goals that reflect a godly purpose. Even though 2010 was filled with chaos, our family learned the power of patience and perfect timing. My hope for 2011 is that we are able to share Brooklyn's story with humility. She's been the greatest gift to our family and I wish to share the joy she's brought us.

Last night the "big move" went well. Brooklyn has been stable most of today and continues to show progress. They have increased her feeds again and have cancelled the nitric oxide. Her chest tube fluid has not slowed down. Every time it seems to decrease, the next day will prove otherwise. Until this fluid gets under control, Brooklyn's swelling will persist. She is still taking intermittent doses of Ativan when needed. The good news is she isn't requiring it as often. Last night she was given a dose at 9 pm. She did not need another until noon today. Brooklyn is fighting harder each day. She is strong, but still needs our committed prayers.

I am positive that, as every New Year, 2011 will bring change. It is my hope that this change will be a positive influence on the purpose our family intends to achieve. Brooklyn has given us one heck of a push start. There's no turning back now.

Bloody Pirate

Freedom rarely comes without a price to be paid.

Some days it feels like Brooklyn is more of a hostage than a patient. Hooked up to machines and glued to so many wires, our girl looks like she's fighting chains half the time. It wouldn't be so bad if she felt no pain, was content the whole time, and could discontinue her distraught demeanor. However, there will be pain, contentment is a challenge, and Brooklyn can break your heart with the faces she makes. It is all a part of the process, I know. That doesn't make this any easier. As a Mother, my instincts to console her are triggered when she becomes upset. It's hard to trust the staff at times. The medical teams are trained to see certain changes and react accordingly, yet they are still human and are capable of missing things. Mother's intuition is both a gift and a curse in this place. Sometimes I can feel so helpless when she's stuck to that bed. I am thankful though that the doctors allow my input during rounds. After all, I am at her bedside daily and may catch something that could easily be bypassed. I have to remember that I am Brooklyn's best advocate. She needs me more than I realize.

Her schedule is jam-packed today. During rounds this morning they decided to bring her morphine down from .06 to .05. This may sound like a small change, but her reaction to it can be big. She did not handle the last wean well, and I can only assume the same for this round. Her feeds have also been increased to 12.5 cc's an hour on continuous flow. She seems to be digesting well and so we will pray this continues on a positive track. From yesterday, the chest tube drainage has cut in half. Before I begin celebrating, I will wait. This has happened in the past, and frankly, I'm a little tired of getting my hopes up. They also seem to think that she will be extubated within the next couple of days. I won't hold my breath. If Brooklyn has taught us anything it's to always be prepared. She's a lot like Jack Sparrow in the sense that you can't completely trust her. There's always a chance that Brooklyn will turn on you last minute. We will be hopeful, but stand alert. It would be thrilling to have the chest tubes removed and the ventilator gone, but like I said, we will be cautious in our excitement.

Guess who's on the move again?

That's right, Brooklyn. She's catching on quick to her parent's tendency to frequently change locations. I would like to say I'm proud, but that would be a false statement. Construction has ended on her side of the NICU so they plan to move her back to C52….two spaces away. Her "sensitivity" and "diva" status is getting old. Miss Princess has the staff at her beckon call anytime there is the slightest whisper of a noise. We love you child, but can you please just pick a bed and stay put?

The doctors need to weigh Brooklyn. The increase in her feedings means that she must be put on the scale more frequently. Today is one of those days. Moving her is always a big deal and the nurse has offered for me to hold her again. If she is not throwing a complete fit at the time, I will give in. Holding her is like a daily goal of mine that never gets reached. I will take full advantage of all opportunities to squeeze that baby girl.

The Lord has been good to us this week. I can feel big changes about to occur and it fills me with much excitement. I pray that all of the alterations in her schedule run smoothly and that she will handle the pressure.

If you're going to act like a pirate sweet girl, than bloody put up a fight.

Stinky Cheese

I was a little disappointed to find Brooklyn's chest tubes back on suction this morning. It seems that they are producing more fluid, and the extra pull is necessary. She appears, however, much more comfortable from last night. The NICU was a madhouse yesterday evening. With the admission of two new babies, it was sincerely loud. Doctors, nurses, and other medical staff rushed to secure peace and order. Backup was called and our girl got bumped from everyone's priority list. I finally had to tell the nurse to give her some Ativan because she was becoming highly agitated with all the chaos surrounding her bed. It's definitely different out here on the floor. Back in the ECMO room, Brooklyn was given prime attention. Now that she's with the regular Joe's, let's just say the chocolate covered strawberries are gone.

Her X-ray from this morning did not bring great news. Unwanted air was discovered in her left chest cavity. They believe this should resolve on its own since the chest tubes are to suction. The doctors really want to see this fluid slack off. These dreaded chest tubes are getting on everyone's nerve endings. They have upped her feeds to 18 cc's an hour since it looks like her stomach distention has come down a bit. Her morphine drip will remain at .05 for a while. Her body must adjust slowly to the weaning process. Spitting up has become repetitive due to increased feedings. This is no real cause for concern except for the "stinky cheese" getting caught in her neck roll. I helped clean this area out yesterday, and let me tell you, it was not pleasant. It would help if Brooklyn were more mobile. Unfortunately, we may not see significant movement for a while longer.

One day this chest fluid will stop. On that day there will be a celebration by Brooklyn's bedside. But until that moment, we sit and we wait. Take your time girl, because we know that's what you will do anyway.

Brain Teasers

"Let the morning bring me word of your unfailing love, for I have put my trust in you. Show me the way I should go, for to you I lift up my soul".

Psalm 143:8

As I'm sitting by Brooklyn's bedside this verse pops into my head. It's one that follows me around it seems, especially when I need it the most. This morning started off with a short mental breakdown. The first bit of troubling news came at 10 am when the hospital called to let me know that some of Brooklyn's medical claims were not being taken by Humana. I'm hoping this is only because they were trying to file it under "baby girl hales" instead of "Brooklyn Elizabeth Hales". This "baby girl" thing comes from the sign they have posted on her bed. Surely the hospital wouldn't think I would name my child "baby girl"... The representative from the hospital said she would re-file under her actual name and see if it goes through. Yes, please try that before giving me a panic attack. As soon as I hung up, another call came through. This time it was from the financial counselor at TCH. Cobra had called her saying that I had not paid in full the premiums for January and so they could not cover the claims sent in. Unaware and uninformed, the premiums had increased January 1st. I was never called with the correct amount needed to send in. After a twenty minute phone call, I finally got the matter settled. Since they sent me the wrong premium amount, they will back pay to the first of the month once I send in the additional cost requirement.

Did I mention how much insurance annoys me?

More unpleasant news came during rounds on Brooklyn. The chest tubes have been accumulating a milky white substance. This liquid is assumed to be fats from her lymphocytes. They are confused as to why this is occurring. Our girl was taken off breast milk and put on the formula Enfaport for this exact reason, to decrease fats. Brooklyn has stumped the doctors once again. Good job girl. I'm not sure why she gets a kick out of confusing the medical staff. It's like she enjoys watching them scratch their heads. Until they can figure out what's going on, they will increase the volume on the formula.

Other than her silly brain teasers, Brooklyn seems to be taking it easy. All that should be required is scheduled maintenance. Suction, diaper change, temp check, repeat.

Recharge

Pardon me while I attempt to get back into the swing of things. Yesterday's break from blogging has created somewhat of a mental road block. I guess it's similar to returning from summer break, your brain needs a little time to regain full functioning. I apologize for leaving everyone in the dark for 24 hours.

To put it plainly, I needed some dog therapy. It had been weeks since I last saw my puppy, and frankly, I was becoming an emotional train-wreck. Having to leave Brooklyn every night to come home has been tough. Not being able to come home to Bella has made it worse. Bad days were always better after an exciting greeting from my four legged child. There is something about that unconditional love that makes your heart happy. Grudgingly, my husband made the trek down to Bay City with me. He needed a different type of therapy called NCAA 2011. Unhappily, he was pulled away from this medicine to keep me company on the drive. I know deep down he was glad to see our dog too, so I didn't feel too guilty dragging him along.

The road trip interfered with the amount of time we got to spend at the hospital, but fortunately Brooklyn had a good day. She didn't sleep a wink, but was content as far as the nurse was concerned. For the brief moments I spent with her she was so alert. I swear there were a couple times she smiled at me. I'm so glad she does not have to receive Ativan as often. You can tell she is starting to actually feel better. One thing that is still concerning though is her edema. From her trunk up, she is increasingly becoming more swollen. The doctors have not yet put their finger on its cause, which is somewhat troubling. This morning an ultrasound has been ordered to explore the option of a possible clot in her neck region. Her time on ECMO may have enabled this blockage and gave way to the accumulation of fluid in her upper body. The medical term for this is thrombosis of the superior vena cava, or SVC. I'm a little unnerved that they are just now checking into this as a possibility. It seems to me that it should be a required examination post ECMO. Whether Brooklyn's swelling is being caused by this phenomenon or another, I hope the doctors figure it out soon. She's been through so much as it is and I would hate for her to go through unnecessary struggles because of overlooked scenarios.

A chest X-ray is also on the schedule for this morning to update us on the fluid situation. Once again, the chest tubes will be taken off suction and put to water seal depending on the status of her pleural effusion. I know this area of concern is redundant, but I feel like we may almost be ready for these annoying tubes to come out. Not to get ahead of myself, but looking at Brooklyn the past couple days has me feeling more optimistic. She is much more aware and active. This leads me to believe she is starting to feel better and growing stronger with each day. We may need to wait a little while longer, but I have a hunch that when she is ready there will be rapid progress.

Hey, we can all hope can't we?

Hope has gotten us this far and so we won't let up. We will gird our loins for the battles ahead, trusting that God will provide the armor.

Happy Plate

Good things always happen when Michelle is our nurse. She seems to think it's just luck; I say Brooklyn likes to show off when she's around. Regardless of the reason, we will take what we can get.

Brooklyn required minimal oxygen and zero Ativan throughout the duration of yesterday. She must have been catching up on her sleep because she was zonked out for the majority of the day. It was just an average day in the NICU until about 6 pm. One of the surgeons came by to check on Brooklyn's tubing because the left side had been producing bubbles. This is usually one of two signs; air in the chest, or the tubing has come too far out. The former was not the desired outcome and fortunately this wasn't the case. Instead, the holes on the end of the tube had come out to the extent that the bubbles were actually just room air. The surgeon undid the dressing and realized the sutures were almost past the end of the gauze holding the tube in place. He decided at this time to remove it. Hey, we will take it! After the tube was removed an X-ray was called in. The left side looked good and they are hopeful the tube will stay out. The right side however, showed some accumulated air. The chest tube was put to suction to try and alleviate this problem.

The results came back from the ultrasound done yesterday to check for any clots. The hematologist found a small blockage in her mid-section, but doesn't believe this is the cause of her upper body swelling. They still plan to put her on a heparin drip to dissolve the clot, and will do an ultrasound in 3-4 weeks. She will need to be on heparin the duration of those 4 weeks. It seems like a long time, but they want to make certain the clot is completely erased.

Hematology will come by later this afternoon to begin the Heparin. An echocardiograph is also on the menu to check the function of Brooklyn's heart. One day at a time is all we know how to do these days. With each sunrise comes a new list of chores on Brooklyn's plate. I'm hoping our girl can make that big plate happy, and devour its contents.

Will It Rain?

It's day 45 here in the NICU at Texas Children's. Brooklyn is sleeping as a result of her Ativan dose given this morning. The doctors have just finished their rounds.

With the left chest tube still out, Brooklyn's pleural effusion is again present. If her X-ray does not show improvement by tomorrow, the tube will need to be put back in. The right side flow has slowed and is now set to water seal. If the fluid can remain unchanged, the possibility of the tube coming out is good. If not, there may need to be changes made to her regimen. When both chest tubes are completely removed, extubation will be attempted.

The go ahead on the Heparin due to thrombus has been delayed. The ultrasound had originally been ordered to see if a clot was causing her upper body swelling. Since the blockage they found was very small and not the cause of edema, the doctors want to wait and see if it clears up on its own. They feel that adding another medication at this time would be a step back in progress.

More scratching of the head occurred as the doctors sat beside Brooklyn's bed to discuss her treatment. They, just as I, are concerned about the constant accumulation of fluid in her chest and the swelling in her neck and face. It's taking Brooklyn quite a while to resolve these issues. Though the doctors don't seem to be extremely worried, you can tell they want to see more progress. Dr. O reminds us all that, "she'll let us know when she's ready", but some of us have a hard time clinging to that patience.

It feels like the calm before the storm. Tomorrow's X-ray will be the determining factor for several things. If it looks good, the surgeons may remove the tube and the doctors will plan for a trial extubation. If it looks bad, the left chest tube will return and our waiting game will continue. Until then, Brooklyn rests. Tomorrow will bring new challenges, but for now our girl can sleep in peace.

Day 45. The calm before the storm.

Forever Indebted

Blessed is defined as bringing pleasure, contentment, or good fortune.

Somehow this word doesn't adequately describe what our family has been given. To express the amount of favor we've received is almost impossible. Speechless is a good term to use because our family is just that, speechless. Over the past six weeks, family, friends, acquaintances and even strangers have taken heart to our daughter Brooklyn's hospitalization. Her story has reached people in a unique way, resulting in a flood of compassion over our precious girl. I wish I could take some credit in her arrival to this Earth, yet I was only a vessel used by God to deliver such a gift. He had a plan for her long before Jered and I had even thought about having a child. (Not that we had thought much anyway before we heard I was pregnant). God seems to stick to His timing even if it's not penciled down on your big chief tablet. Nevertheless, Brooklyn Elizabeth Hales came into this world on November 28, 2010 ready for battle. She amazed us at first with her ability to fight. She captured our hearts when she taught us all about patience, and she continues to soften our spirits with her innate way of bringing people together. She is the definition of a miracle.

How can you appropriately thank God for such an awesome present? Praising Him just doesn't seem enough. Even if I were to continually thank him every minute until my last breath, it would not be sufficient. This same gratitude is what I feel to those who have offered their support in our time of need. The list of people who have followed Brooklyn's journey is exponential and continually growing. We will forever be indebted to our family and friends for making our financial burdens easier to carry. The time and effort to help fundraise is whole heartedly appreciated. Even more credit need be given to those who have so kindly and selflessly donated. Without you, this journey would be much more difficult.

These daily tidbits I share about Brooklyn are all I have to repay this debt. I hope that her recovery brings hope to those who find themselves in times of trouble. I believe her perseverance is a reminder of God's grace and a glimpse into His unending love.

Thank you again from the bottom of our hearts.

Hammer and Nails

My nerves were shot as I sat in the lobby, waiting for my postpartum doctor's appointment. The last time I was there, well, we won't get into that fiasco again ....

My fears were relieved after the exam. Everything looked copasetic, and the doctor assured me I was back to normal. The human body amazes me. How a woman can perfectly be fine six weeks after giving birth is miraculous. I guess it goes to show you that God really does have serious skills.

I am now off from one waiting room to another. I have to admit that it's very convenient having my OB across the street from the NICU. Technically, I don't even have to step outside into this numbingly cold weather. It may take a little longer, but one of these tunnels will lead to the West Tower on Fannin. Surgery is taking place in section C of the NICU, so I will watch some 30 Rock and pay bills in our second living room.

I'm almost certain I missed rounds while I was out, so I'm hoping our nurse took down extensive notes. This morning's X-ray did not show much optimism. It appears that Brooklyn's right lung is again collapsed in the upper lobe. Her pleural effusion seems to have increased as well. In all honesty, I'm a little annoyed with this whole chest cavity teeter totter. Just when we get so close to making some headway, the rug gets pulled out from under us. I'm about to take a hammer and nails to this mobile carpet. I'm hoping the doctors have a different perspective than my current one. Maybe there will be some silver lining in the midst of this chaos.

Once surgery has ended, I will hurriedly go searching for answers. While I wait, I will pray. Brooklyn has surprised us before. Maybe this will be one of those times.

No Schedule

Brooklyn made Nurse Monica work hard for her paycheck last night. With all the changes made yesterday, it must have been one too many for our girl.

She has a few good days and the doctors think they can go crazy. Well, Brooklyn is about to give them a piece of her mind. Late afternoon yesterday they decided to lower her morphine to .03. They adjusted her vent settings to almost nothing in hopes to have her extubated soon. It seems that Brooklyn does not agree with this plan. These changes may have been made too soon. Our girl had a pretty rough night, requiring Ativan as soon as she could have another dose. Since I've been here this morning, Brooklyn's heart rate has dropped five times. A blood gas was drawn and her CO_2 levels are very high. Even though the X-ray did not show significant concern, something is not quite right with our girl.

The doctors decided to round on her after the current ECMO baby. This is always a little scary because they usually begin with the sicker kids and work their way to the healthy ones. Before they rounded, a sample was sent to labs to check for the flu and other rapid illnesses. I won't be surprised when the results come back negative. Even the nurse was surprised the order was put in for the test. She is showing no symptoms of this type of sickness. The doctors have decided to increase her vent settings and try to get her back to her happy place. The right chest tube isn't producing any fluid but I doubt the surgeons pull it while she is in this condition. Her reaction to the changes made yesterday shows us that she's just not ready to move forward.

We know, we know girl; you'll tell us when it's time. No schedule but your schedule, right? We'll try to keep that in mind.

Rabbit Ears

Brooklyn's like a set of rabbit ear antenna; you have to get them just in the right position to make the fuzzy picture visible. This morning our Brooklyn is back in her "happy place". Because of yesterdays fit, Brooklyn's vent settings are back up to where they had been before the drastic changes. This time the doctors are going to take their time weaning, and proceed with caution. If there are any clues to another meltdown they will stop, let her rest a few days, and then carry on. I'm not exactly sure why this wasn't the original plan to begin with. This "new" technique seems much more rational to me.

An order was placed for surgery to take out Brooklyn's right chest tube. Over the past three days, it has produced near to nothing. The nurse's plan is to trip the surgical team when they come by today and make them remove it. I like this plan because it ends with me holding Brooklyn this afternoon. The breathing tube seems to be causing more discomfort for our girl. She has taken on the habit of gagging every few minutes. I know she is probably getting sick and tired of that tube stretching down her throat. With the adjustments to weaning, hopefully within a week or so it'll be out.

This week has had its share of up's and down's, but was kind enough to come and go quickly. I'm excited to say that we have ended on a high note. The weekend always brings a chance for rest, initiating strength for the start of a new week. As God inches Brooklyn closer to the finish line, we continue to give Him credit. Slow and steady is winning this race, regardless of how much we complain about the speed limit.

My Grace Is Sufficient

The sun has set on another day where I did not get to hold my child. A little piece of my heart dissolves every time this promise is broken.

I really believed them this morning when they told me that I would be able to hold Brooklyn once her right chest tube was removed. All the signs were pointing to a happy ending; all the stars were aligning so nicely. I know that it was the right move to put her left tube back in. I know this is the correct choice. What I don't know, or rather understand, is why Brooklyn's body is not absorbing this extra fluid. Weeks continue to go by as the annoyance of Déjà vu repeats itself. Chest tube out, X-ray, chest tube in, repeat. It's like a game of Pac Man, except the little dots multiply for each one gobbled up. A never ending production of little dots. But in this game, the dots are fluid, and the Pac Man is the suction tube.

Every day I wish I could take her place. Unfortunately, this isn't a power we as parents possess. No matter how much I plead and beg, I am still standing while she lies in that bed. But I can hold her hand. I can stroke her head and tell her it'll all be over soon. I can touch her toes and pat her chest, while I whisper words of encouragement in her ear. Just as God places his hand on my shoulder, I can place mine on hers and pray for healing. A soft voice comes from above, reminding me of my daughter's strength. My fears are suppressed as the voice continues to tell me about grace.

> "My grace is sufficient for you, for my power is made perfect in weakness. Therefore I will boast all the more gladly about my weaknesses, so that Christ's power may rest on me. That is why, for Christ's sake, I delight in weaknesses, in insults, in hardships, in persecutions, in difficulties. For when I am weak, then I am strong."
>
> 2 Corinthians 12:9-10

Wail Away

Brooklyn got to show off her new collection of head accessories today during visitation from the Grandparents. Our little cutie did not hold back with her charming display of hand movements and eyelash bats. Her encore consisted of sticking out her tongue, causing a string of "ooo's" and "awe's" to resound.

All in all she had a pleasant day. She met a few new members from her expanding fan club, and relaxed to the sounds of some classical tunes. With the left chest tube in place, her breathing has become more sustained and less strained. The constant pressure on her lungs is lifted as the fluid is extracted. The doctors did not alter anything and instead let the girl rest for a change. Apart from the respiratory therapy, Brooklyn was left alone. Every 8 hours Brooklyn receives what's called CPT (chest physical therapy). During these sessions, small vibrations are administered to the outside if Brooklyn's left chest. Most children find this therapy soothing and enjoyable.

Brooklyn does not.

The girl has great success at being the horse of a different color. Let's just say she threw a pretty decent temper tantrum as the nurse held her hand back and placed the vibrator on her skin. It's a good thing this therapy only lasts a few minutes. I felt bad for the nurse. The way Brooklyn was acting you'd assume the lady was holding a knife in her hand. Our girl calmed quickly after this "torture treatment" was complete. A few pats on the chest, some oxygen increase, and she was back to normal.

The good news is these little sessions are supposed to dissolve the junk in her lungs and get them to expand. If the doctors can tackle this feat, we will be close to getting Brooklyn extubated. My newest goal, apart from holding her, is to finally hear her cry. That girl can wail all she wants and I'll be the one smiling like a fool right beside her. I'm sure a few days of her screams will render me wishing the tubes back in her throat, but for now, I anticipate the cry.

Be ready to put those lungs to use girl. We're ready for you.

Lazy Sunday

My Sunday Fun-day didn't start out so "fun". I was feeling a bit under the weather after dinner last night and still had a touch of it this morning. I decided to choose more sleep instead of attending church. Yes, I needed the rest, but I still felt bad as my husband left for the service.

The rain increased my sour mood as I tromped through puddles to get to my car. Finally making it safe inside, I realized I left my debit card in the apartment. Luckily, I found a few spare dollars to help solve my hunger issues. Fast and furious I pull out of my parking spot only to come to a complete stop. The scraping noise wasn't very promising. With a cringe I turn to my left and realize I'm crammed against the concrete pole. Excellent. With a crunch, I accelerate forward to my original position. Stepping out to see the damage, my stomach sank. Below my left headlight lay a fairly significant dent surrounded by scratch marks.

My nerves settled as soon as I saw Brooklyn. She was so at peace that it immediately released the pressure on my shoulders. The dent in my car quickly became futile. It's amazing how fast she can put things into perspective. Yes it will be a pain to fix my car, and yes it will be an unfortunate expense, but a lot worse things have happened. Instead of being angry, I choose to be grateful. I am grateful for our unbelievably full life. Every day I am taken aback by the amount of love in our circle of family and friends. Without this system of support, I'm certain my optimism wouldn't be so prevalent.

Now as I was saying, Brooklyn is doing well again today. With rounds approaching, I'm interested to see what changes may be in store for her. She's been sound asleep ever since I arrived and comfortably set on 27 percent oxygen. The left chest tube is not producing much fluid, so I assume it will soon go to water seal. If we are lucky, it will come out in the next few days. It looks like it'll be a lazy Sunday for Brooklyn, and I couldn't me more content with that.

Broken Record

Another weekend has passed with no regrets. As we begin a new week, I look forward to reaching new goals. The Big "M" has become a thing to anticipate. Instead of the dreadful "case of the Mondays" feel, this day now brings a fresh start.

Four months ago I would have kicked myself in the shin for saying this, but Monday's have become my new best friend. They are a day where the doctors are regenerated and hopeful. They are almost child-like with their giddy nature, willing to take chances and set new paces. Mondays are a day for change, an opportunity to set new boundaries and push the limits. I realize this has its share of risks involved. As we've experienced in the past, Brooklyn isn't always as ecstatic about reaching these new heights. But with each day she is becoming stronger and more willing to cooperate. One Monday she will be ready, and on that day we will see fireworks fly.

I was a hair shy of making rounds this morning. They had just wrapped up discussing Brooklyn when I arrived at bedside. The morphine has been lowered to .025. Almost there! The doctors do not want to wean this anymore until the left chest tube comes out. The pain it causes requires at least some small portion of medication. Once the tube is removed for good (yes it will happen), then we can really get serious on completely discontinuing her drugs. The surgery team came by earlier to take a peek at her X-ray from this morning. The only note they left was "X-ray looks good, will reassess later". My goal is to actually see someone from the surgical team and get definitive answers. The chest tube isn't producing fluid yet and is still set to suction. Halfway up the tubing looks to be some sort of blood clot. The two observations seem as though they may be connected. The medical staff doesn't seem to be worried, but if the tube isn't working, then what's the point of having it in? Unnecessary pain is not something I can take with a spoon full of sugar.

The NICU is shut down once again for surgery. With my luck, the surgeon will swing by while I'm unable to be back there. Maybe I'll return to answers after lunch. Maybe, just maybe, a choice will be made to remove the tube. This broken record is tired of repeating itself; please come out chest tube.

Pretty In Pink

Chick-Fil-A, you complete me.

I'm surprised there aren't more fender benders coming out of the drive thru at Chick-Fil-A. Pardon the metaphor, but the drivers resemble chickens with their heads cut off as they exit the lot. Anxious to feed their souls, they quickly un-wrap the biscuit or sandwich they just purchased and proceed to devour it. I'm guilty of the same thing. I'm four blocks away from the hospital, but you can guarantee that chicken biscuit is gone before I hit Main Street. Kudos to Chick-Fil-A for successfully making chicken an irresistible breakfast item.

Another unpleasant insurance call woke me up this morning. The hospital is trying to file claims for January, but Humana states that COBRA has not sent the proper information over for our coverage. Looks like another day on the phones.

Fortunately I didn't miss rounds this morning. Don't tell anyone, but I skipped a shower in order to make it to the hospital on time (mum's the word). Brooklyn was sleeping when I arrived. The nurse mentioned her X-ray from this morning looks better than yesterday. I've yet to glance at it so we'll see if she knows what she's talking about. I know this is shocking, but we have another new nurse. I'm still waiting on the promise of consistency for our girl. I know every nurse distributes excellent care, but it's so much easier when they know her past. She's not your typical "by the book" patient. Brooklyn is still set to a .025 morphine drip and stationed between 20-30% oxygen. Her left chest tube is still on water seal, but no output is being recorded. This tube has now been producing near to nothing for three days. I'm hoping the surgical team will make a decision to pull it today.

We are sporting our pretty pink blanket today. I was happy to hear that we can start bringing some of Brooklyn's personal items to make her bed feel more at home. I don't think the nurses quite realize what they've just opened the door to. I will try not to go overboard, but I will be taking full advantage of this opportunity.

Sleep In Heavenly Peace

I woke up on the right side of the bed this morning. For some reason I was just surprisingly upbeat. Nothing extraordinary happened. I didn't win the lottery. I just had this excitement for life and all it entails. Perhaps it was the beautiful clear sky and crisp temperature. Or maybe it was getting to see my baby girl peacefully dreaming and cracking the occasional smile. Nevertheless, joy was present in my heart.

Speaking of dreaming infants, what do you suppose they dream about? I've recently become fascinated with Brooklyn's facial expressions whilst asleep. Whether she's wearing a frown or a grin, you can tell that she is far away in dreamland. Are they dreaming of the time when they were safe and warm in the womb? Or reminiscing the scary experience of taking their first breath? Could it be possible they dream of heaven? Do you suppose God has a hand in their dreams? I like to believe it's the last of these and that our girl is getting a glance at forever. Watching her sleep takes me a step away from reality, and a little bit closer to heaven.

They have yet to discuss Brooklyn's care plan for today, but when they do, I will be ready. Up until now I've been an extremely laid back participant in rounds. I never ask more than a question or two and always agree with the proceeding schedule. Today is a little different. I've decided to start asking questions. They may not be able to answer all of them, but as a parent and Brooklyn's best advocate, I'm entitled to ask. I will ask when they are willing to reintroduce breast milk. I will ask why the chest tube hasn't come out. I will ask when they will try a c-pap instead of intubation. I will ask for a time line.

I will ask, so I pray that they are ready.

I've officially reached my bottle limit at the milk bank. I didn't know this was possible. Bizarre as it sounds, I figured they had infinite storage capabilities. Apparently not. After bringing a load of bottles from the house, one of the lactation consultants politely told me to stop bringing them. She continued to say that

I have maxed out my limit of 150 bottles and should consider buying a storage freezer. I wanted to laugh, but held it in. First, we can't afford to spend money on an appliance of that magnitude. Second, she would be laughing too if she saw the size of our apartment. I guess we could replace the couch with it, but I'm thinking Jered might veto this idea. Our tiny freezer is about to fill up fast. Baby girl better get her gut ready, because this milk needs to start disappearing.

Rounds are approaching. I hope to still be smiling at the end of their discussion.

Do A Little Dance

Good news is impossible to hold in.

I was going to wait until tomorrow to post another update, but rounds went too well for me to suppress the information. The doctors have asked the surgeons to remove Brooklyn's left chest tube. The X-ray this morning looked much improved from yesterday and they believe the drainage is no longer necessary. The surgical team is scheduled to come by late this afternoon for the procedure. The second bit of good news is, drum roll please.....

Extubation to CPAP!

In layman's terms, this means they will take her ventilation tubes out of her throat. In its place, CPAP (or continuous positive airway pressure), will be used to provide oxygen. As stated in a previous post, most kids hate this transition. Even though it's a step forward, Brooklyn may be one unhappy camper for a few days. Until she can become acclimated to the pressure going up her nose, it'll be some rough seas for our girl. The good news is we will finally get to hear her cry. I have a feeling she's going to scare herself with her own voice. Unfortunately, her temper tantrums have been silent up until this point. Finally she will be able to express her anger in an audible fashion. This alone should make her feel somewhat better. Who doesn't like being heard when they scream? Isn't that the whole point of voice infliction?

The doctors have also decided to go down on her morphine from .025 to .02. We can almost smell freedom. It will be a major accomplishment once Brooklyn is able to come completely off this powerful drug. So far she has handled weaning like a champ. Her good friend Ativan has been by her side to make the transition smoother.

It feels like she is finally making significant progress. I'm so in love with this little fighter. She proves time and again that miracles still happen. I thank God everyday for giving us

Brooklyn to remind us of His mercy. With each step she takes toward recovery, I find myself taking a step closer to God. She has inspired my soul to give thanks where it's due. I will forever be grateful for this gift of renewal and strength.

Good news can't be kept silent. Go on, do a little dance.

Dr. Mom

Brooklyn's atelectasis is back….

Her morning X-ray left little room for interpretation. Both top lobes of Brooklyn's lungs are collapsed. Any hope for extubation was crushed as the doctors discussed going up again on her ventilation settings. The good news is they no longer see the pleural effusion that was keeping the chest tubes in. Our girl is finally free from that dreaded drainage system. However, her lungs seem to have taken a toll from the recent chaos and change. For now, Brooklyn will keep her mouth gear. The doctors have ordered CPT to try and expand her lung volume. They have also ordered for position changes every six hours to get her moving. This mobility will help to clear the mucus in her lungs, enabling a greater chance for expansion.

Bad news wasn't the only thing present during rounds. Both volume and calorie count are being increased in Brooklyn's feeds. They believe it's time to fatten her up. With the weight gain, they hope to accelerate her strength and progress. Let's face it; you can't run a marathon on an empty stomach. Her spit-up's have been minimal, so they are optimistic she will excel. Actually, the nurses have been quite amazed by her ability to keep down food. CDH babies are known for their GI and reflux issues. Even when Brooklyn does spit up, the milk is curdled. This means she is digesting the milk almost immediately. Fast metabolism I suppose. I can make an educated guess that this trait comes from me.

Another Ativan was given shortly after 11a.m. when Brooklyn became inconsolable. She seems much more agitated these past few days. The doctors assume it's because of the morphine weans. The look of pain in her face is excruciating. I wish she could at least belt it out. I will be so happy once she is off the drug and no longer feeling effects from withdraw.

I cannot wait until after lunch because the nurse has promised quality holding time. With everything going on I'm thankful that they are keeping their promise. I know being held is just what our baby girl needs to feel better. She needs to be swaddled, squeezed, and loved on. Everyone feels warm and fuzzy after a hug, so that's just what Dr. Mom has prescribed.

Let The Coin Decide

Brooklyn's X-ray looks much better this morning. It seems as if the CPT and frequent rotations are working quite nicely. Both lungs have significant air in them, and the right upper lobe is again inflated. Sometimes I feel like this girl is a one man circus act. You never know what crazy thing she'll do next. Because her blood gas and X-ray were promising, they are ever so slightly coming down on her vent settings. I think the doctors are finally realizing that Brooklyn needs to move more at a snail's pace rather than a gazelle's. The morphine will also be altered tomorrow morning. It currently sits at .02 and will be weaned to .015. Just a splash of her favorite cocktail.

Like clockwork, Brooklyn needed her pal Ativan around 3 a.m. this morning. It's been a few hours since that dose and she still seems to be very content. She's having sweet dreams this morning; cracking a smile between yawns. Getting to hold her yesterday was the highlight of my week. She did incredibly well. At one point during the three hour hold she needed a diaper change. She didn't even flinch. Any other time she would have thrown a fit, but she was too relaxed to care. The nurse even teased that I should be her new Ativan.

I know the grandparents are dying to hold her. I haven't broken the news to them yet, but the nurses only want one hold a day. It's a lot of work to get Brooklyn situated in someone's arms, and until she has her tubes out, they want to limit this process to once a day. Jered decided we'll have to flip a coin. Obviously Nana and Gigi will come before the others, but how are you going to pick which one goes first? Neither of us want to be the one to tell Dianna or Pam "no". So we will let the coin decide.

So far it's been a good morning. Brooklyn is maintaining her oxygen level at 24%, and is still high-stating. Maybe she's just glad it's Friday. I mean c'mon, who doesn't love Fridays?

Thank You For The Peaches

Yesterday felt like looking into a kaleidoscope. With the array of dancing colors, your eye isn't sure where to focus.

Brooklyn finally got a big girl bed. Before we had made our way to the hospital, Nurse Michelle called. Her goal for the day was to transfer our girl from the warming bed to a crib. This meant Brooklyn could start using things like a mobile and her own bed dressings. This alone would have been reason to jump for joy, then came even more excitement. Brooklyn can now start wearing clothes! With the chest tubes out, there's no reason to be stuck in her "birthday suit". It's time to put that closet full of onesies to work. Booties get your game face on; two little feet are ready for some action.

Four days have passed since the removal of Brooklyn's last remaining chest tube. So far so good. An X-ray has been ordered for Monday morning to see how well her body is absorbing any excess fluid. This film will determine the fate of the chest tubes. My hope is that their use will be avoidable and we can throw out the key to the box they'll be stored in. The X-ray will also inform us if Brooklyn is ready for ventilation wean. As long as her lung volume is reasonable, and her blood gas is good, the doctors will slightly adjust her current settings. If Brooklyn continues to show progress, a possible trial extubation may occur. Her morphine drip is down to .015. Soon enough, she will be completely off this medication and one step closer to the removal of her PICC line. This port has been in place since before Brooklyn's corrective surgery. The doctors are anxious to remove this access line because of the risk of infection it possesses. Her body has been strong enough so far to escape this threat, but we will all rest easier once the line is removed.

Another giant step was taken yesterday afternoon when I held Brooklyn "skin to skin". At first I thought the nurse was joking when she told me to remove my shirt in the middle of the busy NICU. But as she rounded up privacy screens, I realized she was quite serious. After stripping down, the nurse placed Brooklyn stomach down on my chest. This was the first time Brooklyn had been in this position. I'll be honest; I was freaking out just as much as she was. But after the initial shock, we each fell into a comfortable rhythm as I firmly pat her back. I can't put into words how good it felt to have her that close. Feeling her tiny heart beat on my chest sent chills down my back. My breath was taken away every time her hand would press against me. She lasted an entire hour before becoming overheated and squirmy. Let me tell you, this girl can produce some body heat. It wasn't 30 minutes before her legs began to sweat. I don't see many footed pajamas in her future.

It's truly amazing to see how far she's come from the days of ECMO. Even though she still has bridges to cross, my husband and I rest easier these days. Our nerves don't shatter every time the phone rings and the tears don't come around as often. One question we get time and again is "how are we handling all of this?" The answer isn't as complicated as you'd think, and in all honesty extremely simple.

God.

Without Him we are nothing. I've recently been in thought about how easy it is to rely on God in times of trouble. In fact, it's often common for faith to remain dormant until something bad happens. When life is "peachy", it's easy to forget about the one who is in control. We all have a way of falling into a routine when the sun shines. When the grass is green on your side of the fence, it's difficult to remember who's watering it. We get prideful, assuming our good fortune is based solely on personal performance. We shouldn't use God as a last resort. He should always come first. Waiting for misery to call on Him is purely selfish. I choose to praise God for the good days and ask for mercy on the bad.

Never forget to thank God for the peaches.

Focus on the Now

Brooklyn's morphine drip is being discontinued today. (Cue dramatic dun, dun, duuun sound).

The doctors are becoming brave and believe our girl is ready to give up her magic medicine. This might get interesting folks. The good news; she's not going completely cold turkey. Every few hours she will be given a bolus of morphine until she is ready to be completely independent. Ativan, of course, will be around in case things get a little messy. Her X-ray showed some pleural effusion in her chest, but not enough to put the tubes back in. The doctors will monitor the fluid with follow-up X-rays and make an informed decision on their absence. Her face is puffier this afternoon due to her change in diuretic dosage. Instead of receiving it via IV, Brooklyn has to take it orally. This means her body must absorb it through the intestinal tract. Because this method takes longer, her body retains the fluid much easier. Until her body becomes acclimated to this change, Brooklyn will suffer from an increase in edema.

I feel spoiled getting to hold her whenever I want. I keep asking the nurse, "So you mean I can just hold my child at any time"? It's a strange feeling really. Mothers usually don't view time spent with their child as a privilege, but in here it is. Holding your child, hearing them cry, and being able to dress them are things of envy in the NICU. Jered and I continually joke about our future children. We aren't going to know what to do when the doctor discharges us from the hospital on day two with nothing but a good luck wave. Now THAT is something to be scared of.

Brooklyn continues to make progress. Today will tell us how dependent she truly is on the morphine. If her X-rays continue to be acceptable, they will discuss further vent weans and extubation. Each day stands alone and can be completely different from the day before. We focus on the now and look forward to tomorrow.

Slim Fast

I should have known better than to wake a sleeping dragon, and by fire breathing lizard I mean Brooklyn.

A photo shoot took place last night as a few friends stopped by to take pictures of Brooklyn. All was going well until I had the bright idea of trying to get her eyes to open. She had been asleep for quite some time and I figured it wouldn't hurt to gently wake her up. I assumed wrong. She did not appreciate the gesture, and proceeded to tailspin into "the dark place". It took much more than a diaper change and strong pat to get her settled. Reinforcements were called in and Ativan was administered. I felt horrible. Not only did I contribute to my daughter's demise, but our company was put in an awkward predicament. Their visitation was cut short, and I was left feeling like a rude hostess.

Brooklyn has had some significant strides this past week, but I must remember that she is still fragile. Where it's usually ok to tickle and pick at a baby, with Brooklyn that's not the case. She is still very sensitive to any type of stimulation. Like I said, I should have known better. I look at it as a moment of weakness. A moment where, just for a second, I believed she was fine. I blame it in part on her cute outfit. She is looking so good these days it's hard to believe she's still sick. I must keep the realization fresh on my mind that we have not left this long and curvy road. There will be forks, dips, and sharp turns.

Brooklyn's episode is suspected to be caused by her fluid retention. Nurse Michelle is a little concerned about why she is not able to pee off all the excess edema. The doctors have ordered an extra Lasix to try and dry her up. Her poor little face is getting more swollen with each day. Her respiratory rate is up as well. A few ideas were tossed about in rounds this morning on attempts to alleviate the swelling. Dr. GP assumes that Brooklyn's anatomy may be the cause of her retention. Because CDH babies begin with their insides in disarray, their bodies must adjust to the new placement of major organs. Brooklyn's capillaries are affected in the midst of these changes and are slow to adjust. Basically it boils down to Brooklyn's body needing time to catch up. We can't expect rapid progress after significantly rearranging the girl's entire GI tract.

The plan for today is to let Brooklyn's "slim fast" challenge take charge. There's not usually a need for diets in the NICU, but our girl doesn't like the norm. Get Jillian Michaels on the phone, our girl needs a quick weight loss regimen.

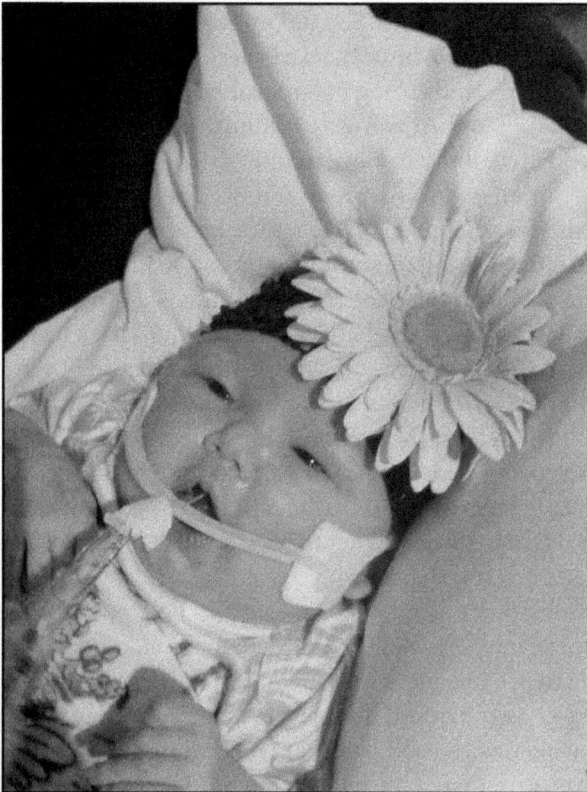

Minefields

Backtrack: to retrace one's course; to reverse a position.

Brooklyn's pleural effusion is back with a vengeance. The accumulation of fluid is too great to just sit and watch. An ultrasound will be done within the hour to determine how bad the situation is. In the meantime, they are stopping feeds. Brooklyn will be taken off the milk drip and put back on TPN. Watching the nurse take down the feed dispenser is rough. Brooklyn has come so far and this setback lands on a heavy heart. The results from the ultrasound will let us know when and if the chest tubes need to go back in. The X-ray suggests that the effusion is at a point where immediate attention is needed. However, the ultrasound may show a different, more detailed view of the problem. Oftentimes, the X-ray can show "false fears". Plainly, it may not be as bad as it looks. Although this may be the case, each face in rounds this morning looked distraught. I've come to find that when the news is bad, I receive less eye contact and more shuffling through papers. Unfortunately, that was the case this morning.

As a result of the increase in fluid, Brooklyn looks extremely swollen. You can tell she doesn't feel well. Even the slightest change in position throws her stats into a downward spiral. Ativan, as well as a dose of morphine, has been given to settle her nerves. She now sleeps peacefully with a chubby little face. It is visible that her body is working overtime to compensate the weight. Her chest rises and falls rapidly, contracting with each breath she takes. If the ultrasound comes back with the worst case scenario, pediatric surgery will be called to put the tubes back in her chest. She will remain off feeds for a few weeks until the doctors believe the issue is resolved.

We had grown comfortable in Brooklyn's progress. I have to be honest that it was a nice break from that state of panic our family had consistently been in. I'm not saying that same panic has returned, but a greater alertness has set in. I guess our girl is reminding us that we must stay on our toes. I wish she would quit pulling pranks on everyone because our nerves have already been thinned.

Even though we find ourselves tiptoeing in minefields, God is guiding our steps. He is gently placing each foot where it needs to land. It is foolish to run where bombs lie, so we cautiously choose our pace. God reminds us this isn't a race. We will follow His lead and be patient.

The Red Zone

My eyes are fixated on a flashing red light. The number reads 87, 64, 50. Where an average of 157 usually shines, digits much lower than that keep blinking. The nurse grabs the green bag and places it over Brooklyn's airway. Squeeze, release, squeeze, release. Her chest expands and falls. My eyes remain glued to the monitor as the number begins to rise. 50, 64, 87, 145. My breath returns and I exhale. Brooklyn's heart rate stabilizes.

The fluid trapped in Brooklyn's chest is so significant that it is compromising her oxygenation. This means she must work overtime in order to get air into her lungs. Every little change sends her stats in a tizzy. She has no reserve. Where a suctioning of her ET tube would result in a slight dip, now has Brooklyn dropping her heart rate for minutes at a time. The fellow placed the order last night for both chest tubes to be inserted. The X-ray had come back and Brooklyn's effusion ranged from moderate to large on each side of her chest. The nurse and I agreed that she needed the tubes in as soon as possible. The release of that fluid is what she needs to help her breath. The doctors however, chose to wait. Her feeds had just been discontinued and they wanted to see if the effusion would decrease as a result of this change. The nurse and I felt that not enough progress would be seen in this short amount of time, and why keep Brooklyn suffering if she needed the drainage. We obviously lost the battle, because here I sit at Brooklyn's side, waiting for her follow-up X-ray.

Brooklyn is going to be sent to the intravenous radiology department for the procedure. This will be the first time she has ever left the NICU. The doctors want to use the ultrasound machine to guide the tubes to a precise location in her chest. The closer they get to the accumulated fluid, the better. She is on significant assistance and is still unstable. The doctors are trying their best to rush the procedure, but the surgery team is packed.

As she lies there helpless, I cry. I cry out of frustration. Frustration from the pleural effusion and its return. Frustration

145

for the doctors and their perplexed thoughts on why this keeps happening. Frustration for not being able to pick her up and make it all better.

Prayer is needed for Brooklyn this morning. She needs one of those deep soul prayers. Many of you know the one I am referring to, the one where your heart aches and planned words aren't enough. The prayer where you find yourself broken before God and only He can give you the words to say. He knows what she needs and I will trust Him. I know our God is with her now, holding her tiny hand. He has never left her side, so I will not leave His.

Unconventional

Today is Brooklyn's two month birthday. The past 30 days have been an absolute blur. During that time, Brooklyn has moved onto the floor, lost her chest tubes, gained her chest tubes, and got rid of them once more. Now, here she faces another chance at having them put back in. The trip to the OR resulted in extracting the fluid via syringes. This process was done in hopes that Brooklyn will not need the permanence a tube insertion brings. So much progress had been made the past ten days that the doctors were talking extubation. But here our girl stands, a few steps back, fighting again the same battles.

Her morning X-ray showed that the fluid is back. However, her respiratory rate is stable and she is only on 20% oxygen. Go figure. The doctors are perplexed by this. All signs show that Brooklyn should be in the same boat she was yesterday. What is this little girl doing to us? The doctors have decided to wait on the chest tubes since she is completely comfortable. They will closely have their eye on her to catch any clues of a dive in stability.

I was pleasantly surprised to see Bridget as our nurse this morning. For weeks we have been trying to get her to primary for Brooklyn. Come to find out, she was nervous to return to our bedside. Once upon a time in the ECMO room, Bridget was carefully changing Brooklyn's lines. In order to reach her properly, step stools had been placed at the foot of the bed. While Bridget was fervently doing her job, her balance became compromised. Stumbling forward, Bridget accidentally tripped over Brooklyn's chest tubes. Her face was ashen and her cheeks blushed as she shamefully looked into my eyes. I could tell she was utterly embarrassed. I however, thought nothing of it. Bridget was one of our favorite caretakers and she deserved forgiveness for her mistake. Apparently she felt so bad about the incident that she stayed clear of our girl until now. Within the first few seconds of talking with Bridget, I remembered why we liked her so much. Within the short amount of time spent with Brooklyn this morning, she had already observed signs of withdrawal.

For the past week, Brooklyn has been sucking on her ET tube. We all assumed this was just her trying to suckle, a normal baby instinct. This is often not the case for infants who have recently come off morphine. Obsessive sucking can be a sign of withdrawal, as well as sweating. Brooklyn has been perspiring ever since they discontinued the morphine drip. A completed assessment reveals that Brooklyn scores a high 10 on the chart. This indicates our little fighter is feeling the results of her missing sedative. Bridget will inform the doctors and have them alter the doses. Brooklyn may need a higher amount more frequently until she can handle the significant wean.

With all this going on our trooper is sound asleep, smiling away. She has successfully peed off some of the excess fluid that had made her face so swollen. She's finally looking more like herself. The fluid in her chest is still a real concern and the doctors will be close at hand. She continues to amaze them with her unconventional way of doing things.

We aren't asking for a whole lot here Miss Brooklyn. If you could try and do something normal for a change it would all help us sleep a little better. We know you like to keep us guessing, but it's time to try and follow a more predictable line.

We love you more than life you crazy girl. Happy 2 months!

Broken

Mother's intuition should never be underestimated. That invisible line between Mother and child was once unfamiliar territory. Now, these unmistakable feelings I have for Brooklyn are not only present, but unshakable. I think it's an even stronger bond between mother and daughter. Game night proves this theory right in my family. No matter what attempted shape my Mother creates with the Cranium dough, I never fail to know exactly what she is trying to imitate.

Last night this telepathy kicked into gear. Around 10 pm I felt the urge to call and check up on Brooklyn. I usually never call at night, trusting the nurse will call with anything significant. The nurse informed me that everything was fine and our girl was sleeping soundly. I trusted her answer, but still felt unsettled throughout the night. This morning I found out that my fears were not so irrational. Around midnight Brooklyn had an episode where, regretfully, the green bag had to show its ugly face again. Our girl was able to push through and stand firm on stable ground, but this fluid is plucking away at everyone's spirit. Her morning X-ray painted another unfortunate picture. The right lung is significantly compromised due to the pleural effusion. If Brooklyn wasn't so stable, the chest tubes would have already found themselves tucked back into the unhealed wounds of Brooklyn's side. Somehow our little fighter is trying to prove science wrong, defying the numbers on paper.

Miss B continued to tug on our emotions when she decided to extubate herself this afternoon. In a fit of agitation, Brooklyn slipped a finger through her tubing and proceeded to pop a cheek guard off. This lack of containment caused the ET tube to slip out. Brooklyn went from bad to worse, forcing the medical team to re-intubate her. The afternoon followed this bumpy path into early evening. Brooklyn was impossible to comfort, requiring more oxygen, morphine, and Ativan. Our baby girl had entered her dark place. Contentment had flown the coop. What made things worse were our attempts to soothe her. We didn't realize it, but we were over stimulating her with our strokes, pats, and whispering words of encouragement. It was too much for her and she became smothered.

It was hard enough she was upset.

To know that we added to her stress was worse.

Not being able to cradle and rock her...to tell her everything will be ok....broke me.

God eased our pain this evening when she finally found that resting place. I know our girl will have these moments of weakness. I've been a witness many times to their show. But I will never be prepared for them. I will never be a good hostess to their visits. What I can be is ready to lean on our God. I can be ready to call on His name and beg for mercy. I can break my heart in His presence, knowing that this too shall pass.

I can...and will....pray.

The Leader Of The Pack

Attempting to hold back tears during worship yesterday was like trying to stop a speeding bullet. I had become so emotionally drained that my body was automatically reacting. There is usually a song in the lineup whose lyrics parallel or relate to Brooklyn's situation. God always seems to show me a clip of what he is creating out of our desperate circumstance. One phrase that kept repeating itself within me was:

"You use the weak to lead the strong"

I immediately thought about how Brooklyn continues to lead us through her journey. How, through her weakness, she shows us how to rely on God and build our faith to what He can accomplish.

I cannot wait for the doctors to start her feeds again. This cry face is slowly breaking me down. The morphine and Ativan have been increased to help calm her and promote comfort. Her belly isn't fooled by the sidetracking. It knows it is empty, and will continue to let us know. Even in her sleep, Brooklyn is cranky. I know the purpose of this forced diet is to help her absorb the fluid in her chest, but I wish the process wasn't so drawn out. The past couple of days have left my patience dangling from a very thin thread. I fear the next hiccup could result in a snap and fall.

Brooklyn's next X-ray is scheduled for Wednesday. This will hopefully show that Brooklyn's body is finally starting to absorb this extra fluid. If the progress continues, the doctors can reintroduce feeds in about a week. Also in the works is an order for an MRV. This scan examines the veins in Brooklyn's upper body to determine their function. The mystery of her edema still remains. This test will ultimately give the doctors a better understanding of Brooklyn's anatomy in hopes to settle the swelling issue. Dr. GP will discuss this option with radiology and decide when to proceed with the scan. I'm very interested to see the results and perhaps gain insight to this constant problem.

Brooklyn may currently be in a state of weakness, but it hasn't stopped her from being a leader. I feel honored to be one of her followers.

Thank you Father for prayer. Thank you for a brokenness that forces us to bear our souls to you. Thank you Lord, for those precious moments where I see clearly that it's not about me.

Merry-Go-Round

Around, around, around we go. When we'll stop, no one knows.

The start of February brings new faces to Brooklyn's bed space. Dr. GP has moved on to another rotation and in his place sits Dr. W. We briefly met with Dr. W when Brooklyn was in the ECMO room. Although he has rounded on her before, this will be his first time as Brooklyn's primary physician. He made a very good first impression during this morning's discussion. It was one of the few times a doctor had actually gone to the bed side to examine Brooklyn. It's hard to believe, but doctors have come and gone without even looking at Brooklyn. There are many who rely heavily on the nurses and other staff to inform them of changes in behavior. I was thrilled when Dr. W even tried to console Brooklyn as she squirmed making the cry face.

The problem is this cycle she's caught in. If her body could get a handle on the pleural effusion situation she would make exponential progress. Once the fluid is absorbed, she can begin eating. Once she begins eating, she can grow. Once she starts growing, she will get stronger. And once she is stronger, the faster she can heal. We are currently losing the effusion battle. The doctors are doing everything in their power to keep the chest tubes out. With the tubes in, Brooklyn's body will continue to produce the excess fluid. Unfortunately, her body can only take so much accumulation before drainage needs to happen.

This Merry-go-round is getting old.

I could wait forever if Brooklyn was happy and comfortable, but this is not the case. She is hungry and upset. The hardest thing I've done yet is to watch her cry for food and not be able to feed her. Brooklyn's frustration as to why we aren't listening to her is heart wrenching.

I pray that God would give her the feeling of a full stomach. That she would no longer feel pains from hunger, but be full with His spirit. I pray her body begins healing and the fluid is absorbed. I pray for my sanity and hope it holds on. Amen

Skim Milk

Milk is said to do a body good. You never hear TPN having a slogan like that. Yes it's the choice for alternate nutrition right now, but one would think after a week of worsening X-rays, a better idea would have been revealed. This is the Texas Medical Center for crying out loud. Isn't it similar to NASA where they have people sitting around just thinking stuff up?

During rounds this morning, the idea of bringing feeds back was tossed around. The NPO (nil per os, or nothing by mouth) diet has proven ineffective. Brooklyn's X-ray was obviously worse and talk about a medication called Octreotride was discussed. Dr. W prefaced this option by saying he's never seen it work in any of the CDH babies he's treated. Even in healthy babies the percentage of success averages only 30%.

Very encouraging . . . . .

While the subject of feeding was occurring, I decided to throw my two cents in. GiGi had found an article about a boy who suffered from pleural effusion and chylothorax just like Brooklyn. At one point during his fight, he had to endure four chest tubes. The doctors struggled with this boy and his treatment, similar to Brooklyn's circumstance. The Mother had read about how the La Leche League can "skim" breast milk. She believed this was worth trying and brought it to the medical team's attention. The underlying issue with chylothorax is the lymph system's inability to break down fats. With this skim milk, the fat is cut down or extracted from the original product. Needless to say, this idea worked. After the feedings began, they started seeing progress right away.

I was brave enough to bring up this possibility in rounds this morning. I was pleasantly surprised when it wasn't immediately shot down. Dr. W pondered this for a moment and then informed me that he had never heard nor thought of doing this. They have had cases where milk needed more fat, but never less. He told the nurse practitioner to check with the milk bank to see if this could be an option. He said it was worth looking into, and it could only help.

Good. My job here is done making sure the doctors cover all angles. Sheesh.

Little Miss Cranky Pants is still hungry. While in the middle of soothing her I found my million dollar idea. A patting machine. If I were to stand here all day and pat Brooklyn, she'd be one happy camper. Unfortunately, my arm only has so much stamina and cannot withstand a 24 hour workload. Enter patting machine. This state of the art, nonexistent item will be one hot commodity among NICU's. Every bedside will want this top of line crib attachment.

Now all I need is a few thousand dollars for engineering and production costs…. No biggie.

Until the patting machine hits the shelves, I guess I'm stuck with the conventional method of manual patting. It's OK girl, you are worth the early onset of arthritis.

Leaky Pipes

1 out of 3000 babies is born with CDH. 50% of these infants require ECMO. 7-28% of CDH babies develop chylothorax. Of the patients with chylothorax, majority are treated and healed with drainage and diet. The small remaining group of kids needs another surgery to seal off the thoracic duct....

Guess which category Brooklyn is flirting with?

Yesterday evening while I was holding my baby girl, Sanjiv from pediatric surgery came by. I could tell by his demeanor that he was bringing sour news. He stooped down and rested his arm on the recliner we were seated in. He went on to explain that he had seen the last X-ray and regretfully admitted it didn't look improved. The doctor's efforts to clear Brooklyn's chylothorax with cutting feeds and inserting chest tubes have been unsuccessful thus far. If the Octreotide does not produce results, the next step is surgery.

The thoracic duct lies adjacent to the esophagus and next to the aorta. It is the main component of the lymphatic system. There have been several instances where this duct is mistakenly tampered with during surgery, much like that of a hernia repair. The surgeons believe this leaking duct may be the root cause of Brooklyn's "leaky pipes". There are instances where the body can heal this leak on its own without intervention. Brooklyn is telling us she may not be able to do it alone.

We haven't given up yet. This morning during rounds the doctors implied that they want to wait at least two weeks before making a decision on surgery. They want to give the medicine plenty of time to prove itself legitimate. Therefore, we find ourselves sucked back into the waiting game. Brooklyn will continue to get X-rays every few days to monitor the chylothorax. As long as she remains stable, we will sit patiently over the 14 day span.

With all faith we remain hopeful that the fluid will be absorbed and surgery will not be necessary. We cling to our prayers for restoration and healing in Brooklyn's chest. Continuing on this rollercoaster, we rejoice on our way to the top, and hold on for dear life during the falls.

Little Ali

Yesterday was a good day. I even found myself saying this out loud to my husband as we laid our heads down last night. He had taken the day off due to our "snow day", and therefore was privileged to spend some time with Brooklyn and myself. We even made a trip to the galleria (gasp). Neither of us had been there in ages and it felt good to get outside of our hospital life for a moment.

Brooklyn slept through the majority of yesterday, which made it easier to leave her side. I'm trying my hardest to break the feeling of guilt I have when I'm not in the NICU. It's unfortunate that I take on this sense of abandonment when I'm not with her. I know she is in good hands, but at the same time I feel lost when I leave. The hospital has in some ways become our home. Being distanced from her just feels wrong.

Sanjiv from surgery stopped by again to check on Brooklyn. He told me that he doesn't want to do the thoracic duct procedure on her. What he would love to see is her effusions clear up, and then he can take a half day. He reminded me of how far she has come. His tone had a sense of adoration. Brooklyn has become like family to most of the NICU staff. They cling to her progress like a squirrel to a telephone cable. Each nurse and doctor that cares for Brooklyn rides the same emotional train we do every day. You never know what it's going to be with this one. She'll surprise you every time. Just when you think you've figured her out, she'll change your mind. Sanjiv and I both agree that once this fluid is taken care of we will see her flourish. It's amazing how well she is doing given this setback. Brooklyn still remains on 20% oxygen. Even though her lungs are struggling to expand from the chylothorax, she is pressing through. It's almost as if she is saying, "What fluid?"

We don't want our little Ali getting too cocky. She may be handling the pressure well, but she's not out of the water yet. Her X-ray this morning showed no change. It may not be worse, but it hasn't improved either. They have increased her dose of Octreotide while the waiting continues. As always, we anticipate the Lord's intercession in her recovery. Our hope endures as we patiently sit tight to see better results. He is faithful and continually mindful of our needs. Therefore we know, in His time, Brooklyn is healed.

A Humming Heart

Sometimes my heart hums.

No, I don't have a murmur. My anatomy is not irregular, and the beating function is just fine. The part of my heart that hums is the same part that speaks to God; only it hums when it can't find the words to say. It hums when it's stuck between several different emotions. It hums, until it can regain recognition of what it's trying to achieve. Praise, fear, gratitude, guilt. My heart hums when the threads of these words get intertwined and tangled.

It hums when the weight gets heavy.

And even though my heart hums in an unfamiliar tune, God deciphers its plea.

That's the great thing about the Lord. He doesn't need a map or outline to know where your heart is at. He doesn't need special tools to figure out what it needs. Instead, he listens to its hum, and reacts accordingly.

Brooklyn was sleeping when I stopped by before church this morning. She woke up briefly, only to yawn and shut her eyes again. Another X-ray will be done tomorrow as the medical team anticipates a change in Brooklyn's chest. We join the rest of the families in the NICU while we wait for good news. Many days it's hard to find patience and understanding as we've come to realize this past week.

Today I ask you to pray for two families, one of which had to say goodbye to a boy named Connor. Please pray for healing in the hearts of his parents and family. Pray for their support and encouragement in this desperate time. I also ask that you lift up Ella Rose. Ella is Brooklyn's neighbor in the NICU. She was born with all of her intestines on the outside of her body. She has already had her corrective surgery, but unfortunately lost 80% of her bowels. She was doing very well until she was thought to have Meningitis yesterday. She has been put on antibiotics and moved into a solitary room. Please pray for her fast recovery. Pray that she be completely healed and any long term effects would not be an issue.

My heart hums for Brooklyn and these families. Join me if you will, in one big hum to heaven.

All Who Are Weary

Brooklyn's X-ray was BEAUTIFUL!

It didn't even look like the film of the same child yesterday. Both lungs were full of air and only a small portion of fluid could be seen. The doctors have ordered an X-ray for next Monday. If her chest still looks this good or better, they will begin feeds! A week seems like a long time, but the doctors aren't taking any chances. They want to be positive that Brooklyn is finally on the right track. The hard part is not knowing whether the results are from NPO or Octreotide. Dr. W was in shock as he gazed intently at the computer screen. He even double checked the name on the slides. In his years of working with CDH infants, he's never seen the medication work. He is still skeptical, and waiting to make sure we don't get a "surprise" sometime this week.

Brooklyn is also completely off Morphine and Ativan. The doctors have discontinued both drugs in hopes that Brooklyn can now be calmed without them. This is another giant leap. So far she seems to be taking it well. Her temper tantrums are becoming shorter, and her stats rarely drop to nerve-racking levels.

Brooklyn has developed some sort of eye goop. Her right eye currently leaks a yellow pus-like substance. Because of its color, the doctors hope it is merely a clogged tear duct. Precautions have been taken and tear drops were ordered in case it may be something more. Signs of color change and swelling will be monitored to determine if additional care needs to be given. In the meantime, cotton balls of sterilized water are Brooklyn's new enemy. She absolutely hates this routine in her schedule. However, I'm glad they recognize the potential threat and are taking protective measures.

I ended my good day on a high as I joined my sister-in-law in a yoga-esque fitness class. Even though the only thing I proved was that I'm terribly out of shape, I very much enjoyed the relaxing atmosphere. With each long inhale and exhale, I could feel my stress melt away. At the end of class, the instructor read a passage from her devotional as we sat on the floor with our eyes closed. It couldn't have had a better theme.

"Come to me, all you who are weary and burdened, and I will give you rest." Matthew 11:28

The devotional went on to remind us of the power of Hope. As the hour came to a close, the instructor encouraged us to lay our burdens down. God is bigger than anything we struggle with. He can handle the weight. When we Hope in Him, we become vulnerable, asking Him to take over in the areas of life we cannot handle.

It was a perfect ending to the day. The X-ray was a reminder that Hope is enduring and God hears our cries. He is faithful as long as we remain faithful.

The Big Bang

Fast and furious is a dangerous strategy when dealing with Brooklyn. For those who see her on a daily basis, we know she calls the shots. She will shock you, confuse you, and sometimes make you run for cover. I assumed the doctors had learned from past mistakes; that getting ahead of themselves is easy with this one. I thought, as a group, we had come to the realization that this girl doesn't take rapid change well.

Yet here we are, watching the ventilation settings drop at a phenomenal pace.

Granted, Brooklyn is taking it on like a rock star. So far she has had outstanding blood gases. Our nurse Michelle joked that she's going to start hiding the results from the doctors so they ease up in this race of weaning. Dr. W wants her tubes out. He believes she is ready, and thus proving it by taking the changes so well.

I remain hesitant, and for good reasons I might add.

I know not to test this child. She always seems to be on an agenda much different from everyone else. I want her extubated as much as the next Joe, but I also want to dodge setbacks. Rushing into things often leads to unsteady feet. We must stay alert on Brooklyn's shaky ground.

The plan for the next 24 hours is to continue inching our way down on Brooklyn's PIP and PEEP settings. Every 3-4 hours, a blood gas will be drawn. If the CO_2 levels are acceptable, each of these dials will be turned down 1. She is currently set on a PIP of 24. Once that number hits 19, they will discuss extubation.

This is both exciting and scary. I have faith that our champ is ready, I just hope she shares this faith. The cannon is loaded, and the igniter is lit. I'm more than ready to hear her big booming cry.

Drum roll Please

Stretched to their full capacity, my eyes were open as I laid my head down last night. It felt like I was five again and it was Christmas Eve. The anticipation was eating me alive as I sat ever so patiently waiting for Santa to climb down the chimney. But it is not Christmas Day. There are no presents under a tree, and all our cookies have remained untouched. However, the excitement is all too familiar as the hours continue to pass.

75; the number of days our girl has been with us, without a chance to cry. 3.5; the number on Brooklyn's ET tube which has been lodged down her throat. 20; the number we must reach before we hear that sweet sound of her voice.

I think Brooklyn realizes how close she is to being extubated. Every chance she gets to try and escape the tube she takes it. I'm actually impressed by some of her tactical moves. Whether it's arching her back as far as she can, or sneaking up that right arm, she is determined to get her freedom.

Our girl currently sits at a PIP of 21 and a PEEP of 5. In 10 minutes they will draw a blood gas. If the numbers are good, Brooklyn will reach that goal the doctors are looking for. Her stats are perfect, and she sleeps at peace. Her face is no longer swollen, and she wears a grin with her tiny lips. She knows it is time. Once the doctors make their rounds, a decision will be made.

Drum roll please.....

It's about to get loud.

Free At Last

Adrenaline has been pumping through my veins all day. I found myself anxiously pacing back and forth as we waited for the respiratory team to take out Brooklyn's ET tube. Excited, scared, nervous, and joyful, my heart raced with anticipation. Would she be able to breathe on her own? Was she strong enough? Would she scream at the top of her lungs? Would I cry at the sound?

All questions were answered as the tube slowly emerged from her little mouth. She was breathing on her own. Her lungs were strong enough. With all her might she tried to scream, but only a whisper came out. I was too shocked to cry as I stood in amazement at my precious baby girl. She was stunning.

The day was a blur after that. I held her until my arms went numb, and then I held her some more. Over the shoulder, standing up, in the chair, and at her bed. I rocked, patted, and snuggled with my girl. It. Was. Awesome. Pure bliss is the only way to describe today. Every facial expression she made was new and exciting. She has yet to disappoint with her sassy attitude. One small pucker of her lips and my heart melts all over again. Everyone we knew would stop by to give their congratulations. There was a party going on at C52.

Brooklyn has yet to sleep one wink. She's probably afraid that if she drifts off she'll wake up with tubes back in her throat. Heck, I'd keep my eyes peeled for that too. Each time her eyes begin to close she jumps. She is skeptical of every move we make. Her only contentment is found by vigorously patting her back, continuous rocking, chair vibrations, or all three. Usually it's all of the above. We wouldn't want to make things too simple now would we? She gets so mad when she finds out that she's fallen asleep. Her lack of strength to keep her eyes open appalls her. It's as if she's telling herself, "How dare you give in"!

I was quite relieved when Dad showed up. If this is a precursor to what we will deal with at home, I'll admit I'm a little terrified. I keep telling myself that if we lived through ECMO, we can do just about anything. Bring it on baby girl, we need the challenge. You've been making things too easy on us lately.

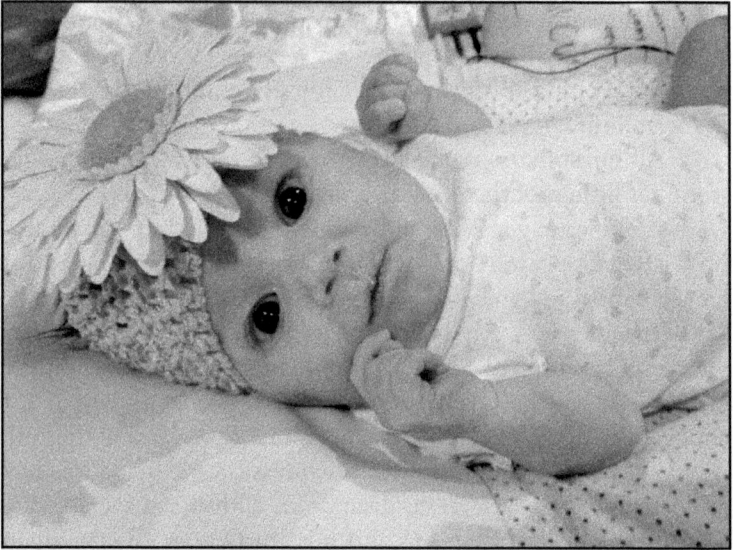

A Story Continued

Brooklyn has decided to try her hand at breaking the world record for staying awake. The current record is 11 days, or 276 hours. Let's hope our little insomniac finds rest before then. It's not that she hasn't tried. The child is out of her mind exhausted. She just knows that once she closes those little eyes, a piece of this, "whole new world", will be lost. In all honesty, I think she was finally able to catch those hard to find zzz's after her visitors left last night. It just would have been rude to check out with company present.

I am ecstatic about her achievement. She has astounded us all with her ability to come off the ventilator without any major hiccups. She's such the little show off, and I almost feel guilty basking in her glory. I couldn't be more proud when the doctors walk by and say, "Wow, she looks great". God has outdone himself. These significant strides encourage our calloused knees as prayers are being answered.

For those who have asked, there is no timeline of when Brooklyn will come home. Yes, she has made so much progress, but there are still challenges ahead. Next week her primary physicians will talk to the surgery team about starting feeds again. Unfortunately, we do not know if the chylothorax has subsided due to her being NPO, or if it is a result from the Octreotide. Brooklyn will need to handle the milk without the return of pleural effusions. If the Octreotide is doing its job, this should not be an issue. Nonetheless, if the fluid returns, there is always a chance that Brooklyn could be reintubated. I say this, not to be pessimistic, but to give a realistic view of what our girl is up against. We thank God every minute for her sudden success, but remain alert for what the future holds.

Thank you for the continued support in this journey. We love sharing each milestone with Brooklyn's followers, and will continue to do so until she makes it home. We are ultimately thankful for our Father in heaven for blessing our lives with such an amazing gift. I will forever be amazed that we were chosen to walk this path. It has been long and sometimes weary, but also extremely rewarding. I consider our family very blessed to tell this story.

Empty Belly

"Everything rides on hope now. Everything rides on faith somehow. When the world has broken me down. Your love sets me free."

—Addison Road

What a perfect song to start the new week. I love the last line. It inspires me to remember that no matter what I am going through, His love can set me free. God has been good to us these last few days. Brooklyn is making everyone's jaw drop in awe at her progress. You can really begin to see her personality shine through. I know I've helped in giving our girl her sassy reputation, but believe me, she does well enough on her own. She is such a mess. Her face will be turning red as she cries in her crib, but the moment you pick her up she is completely content. Spoiled much? So be it. I'm pretty sure there is a line that stretches to Alaska of family and friends waiting to hold her. This child will never learn to walk.

Ok, so now to the nitty gritty. Brooklyn's X-ray has not improved since last week. It has not digressed, but still is at a point where the doctors do not want to proceed with feeds. It looks like Brooklyn will go another week on an empty belly. She is doing so great, but the physicians feel moving ahead will cause more harm than good. Dr. W will discuss the matter further with surgery to expose their insight. I trust that they will come to a consensus that best suits Brooklyn and her needs. Patience will be crucial again as we wait.

On a happy note, Brooklyn has a photo shoot scheduled for this afternoon. She's decked out in her pink heart onesie for Valentine's Day. I must say she is rather adorable. I can't wait to see how the pictures turn out.

Thin Mints Anyone?

It feels so good to be typing on a full keyboard. My index finger thanks me for the vacation. I'm pretty sure my pointer could win some type of wrestling contest if one existed outside of thumb-war. From day one my iPhone has been the distributor of each update. Yet today, I sit in an office chair behind a desk. Yes, you read correct, I'm at work.

When Gary called and asked me to sit for Myrna while she was out, my immediate response was, "Yes"! I had fallen into this self loathing feeling due to my non-contribution to our income. I've always had a job, and to feel unproductive is very unpleasant. However, leaving the hospital to come downtown was a bit harder than I thought. I'd become accustomed to the freedom of seeing Brooklyn whenever I wanted. The main thing holding me together is the fact that Michelle is her nurse today. I know she's in good hands. Arriving at the temp agency this morning to sign papers I felt alive. I was returning to this "business world" that had been forgotten. My confidence shrank as the lady behind the front desk pulled out her wallet. She thought I was a girl scout coming to sell cookies….. C'mon lady, just when I was feeling good about myself. I even have work clothes on today. Talk about a kick in the shin. I guess I can't be completely discouraged. I've just given birth and still look like an adolescent.

I woke up extra early so I could hold my baby girl this morning. I'll be working 12-5 each day which still gives me the opportunity to sit in on rounds. The doctors have decided to increase Brooklyn's feeds from 4 cc's to 8 cc's. So instead of one teaspoon, our girl gets two now (insert sarcastic tone). Full feeds will come eventually, but we must be patient. Shocking Brooklyn's system is not something we want to do. As seen in previous encounters, she needs these baby steps. She will run in due time, but first let's take a stroll in the park. Did I mention that these feedings I speak of are actually my milk? I can't begin to tell you how excited I am about this. Because Brooklyn is on the Octreotide, breast milk is the preferred choice. Formula is digested more slowly than breast milk, and can increase the risk of certain side effects when used with the medication. Even though breast milk contains a heavier fat content, it is easier on the stomach and a more beneficial option. The doctors are hoping this combination of Octreotide and feeds will allow Brooklyn to be nourished without reaccumulation of the chylothorax. If the fluid returns, alterations will be required. If the pleural effusion gets worse, Brooklyn may need to be put back on Enfaport.

As of 12 noon today, Brooklyn had her first bottle! I can't believe I had to miss it. She will have a feeding every three hours, so I will be there for the 6 o'clock chow time. I cannot wait to see how she reacts. Until today, she has never tasted anything but sucrose. Watching her taste milk is going to be incredible. I'm filled with so much joy as I watch her progression. She acts more and more like a normal child each day. I can't believe how much growth she has made these past couple of weeks. It truly amazes me how far she has come. We've been climbing this mountain for 79 days. The top will soon be reached, and we can start our sprint coming home.

Good News Streak

Jered has caught the flu.

I guess my repetitive pleas to get his shot weren't quite forceful enough. Either that or there must have been a short circuit in my broken record. What is it with fellas and their highly acute sense of absenteeism? Sometimes I feel like I should walk up to him, knock on his forehead, and ask; "Hello, Anybody home"? I am now trying to quarantine him within our tiny apartment. He has successfully contaminated every square inch of our bed; therefore, I now reside on the couch. I need a mosquito plane to spray Lysol over the 500 square feet of this place. There's no way I'm getting out of this unscathed. I feel like a contestant on survivor. I'm actually thinking about taking on the swine flu fashion statement and wear a mask around.

This morning I made sure to be cautious around Brooklyn. Any hint of a sneeze or cough and I was ready to bolt. She was sound asleep when I arrived. Every few seconds her body would jump. Her arms would stretch over her head and her eyebrows would rise up really high. Her eyes were too heavy to open but you could tell she was trying hard to wake up. I missed rounds because of an appointment I had scheduled with the Social Security Office. Fortunately, I got to feed her before leaving. She did so great! I sat with her for a good thirty minutes, but she finished every drop of the 4 cc's. This amount is such a tease. I know she can handle more and so I hope the doctors increase the portions today. Nurse Michelle has asked the occupational therapist to come by later this afternoon to assess Brooklyn. We need to gain a better understanding of her actions at feeding time. The therapist can clue in on certain behaviors that will give us insight to any aversions. Brooklyn seems to not be interested when liquid comes out of the nipple. She also has a pretty prominent gag reflex. Rose (the OT) may be able to do some exercises with her that will promote successful feedings.

Brooklyn will get an X-ray in the morning to determine how her effusions and possible atelectasis are coping. Depending on the results, Dr. W will decide if the current plan of action is sufficient. I pray for another beautiful picture. There is such a feeling of relief when that film pops up and her lungs are full of air. I've become quite the expert at deciphering the X-ray data. I can pinpoint areas of concern and know what each haze signifies. It's interesting how fast I can learn things when it involves my child. I've surprised myself many a time when it comes to her care. I don't think I'll ever forget some of the terminology I've had to repeat over the last few months.

We are still on a "good news" streak. I hope to continue these light hearted posts until our girl comes home. Thank you for the continued support and prayers. As always, we are so grateful for Brooklyn's following. We anticipate the upcoming BBQ benefit and are excited to thank people face to face. It's going to be an amazing event and I hope everyone is able to come and have some fun!

A Raspy Warrior

That beautiful cry we've been waiting on may not come for a while.

Brooklyn's right vocal cord has partial paralysis. She had been intubated for so long that the ET tube caused some slight damage to her throat. The glands above her vocal chords are also swollen. It could take weeks before either of these heals. The ENT team did a bronchial exam to verify these outcomes. Another throat scan will be attempted in three weeks to compare the findings. There is a strong possibility of the paralysis clearing up. However, long term effects have been seen in some cases. Weakening of the cords can cause feeding issues among others. Brooklyn is already up against some mild aversions, and this new development may only add to her feeding challenges. The Occupational Therapist came by to administer Brooklyn's lunch. She worked with her oral motor skills and sucking abilities. She told me it would be a long and frustrating road, but if we are patient, Brooklyn will eventually take the bottle quite well. She has no problem taking the pacifier, but when liquid is involved, she gags and sputters. This is most likely the result of both the ET tube being in so long, and prior reflux episodes. Swallowing is difficult and unpleasant for our girl. It will take a lot of time and effort to make feeding time an enjoyable experience.

The doctors are also a bit concerned about her growth chart. Where a climbing line should be, a plateau exists. Brooklyn is currently receiving a high amount of calories without the payoff. For now, they will continue to monitor her progress. If it continues to be a concern in the future, a meeting with surgery will take place to discuss other options. This news is being placed on the back burner right now. Dr. W says there are more pertinent issues we must deal with before moving in that direction. Brooklyn's X-ray still shows some mild chylothorax in her left chest cavity. As long as the effusions do not worsen, we are fine. Milk has been increased and an X-ray is scheduled for next Monday. Our fighter is working hard to achieve those desired full feeds.

Our raspy warrior has some hefty battles to face. She has proven to be an all-star in previous tasks, and I'm sure this time will be no different. As God guides her tiny steps, I lift up my praises for each success. This rocky road doesn't stand a chance against Brooklyn's bulldozer.

MJ Hales

Rolling sea fog covers the Texas coast this morning. The moist droplets circulating in the atmosphere have it feeling like a sauna. The 60 degree reading on whether.com is misleading. Thickened air has my body working hard to pump oxygen into my lungs. It's a nice workout just getting to my car. In this thought process I stop to think of Brooklyn; her tiny lungs and their rough start in life. Simple tasks like breathing have a whole new meaning to me. Taking in the thick air I smile. My daughter has conquered every struggle that has come her way. The inspiration she gives me is beyond words. My eyes have been opened to how awesome this life we've been given is. I thank God for all he has done and continue to be mindful of his mercy.

Jered heads back to work on Monday and couldn't be more ready. He got a taste of how feeding time goes with Brooklyn and has decided I should get more credit for patience. It is a struggle I'll admit, but worth all efforts. I know our girl has what it takes to overcome the challenge. Her aversions are grand, but our God is grander. He is bigger than any gag reflex, and more ferocious than any oral malfunction. It's only a matter of time before Brooklyn gets the hang of swallowing, and then I'll be under pressure on the whole milk production bit. If the girl is anything like her daddy, she won't hold back at mealtime.

A low-key weekend is planned for Brooklyn. Her only tasks are to keep working on feeds and maintain her adorable charm. Sit, be cute, and don't give the nurses a hard time. She has plenty of people wrapped around her finger, and the list continues to grow. Her entourage is beginning to challenge that of Michael Jordan. It'll be one more miracle on our tab if she comes out with some humility.

Straight Paths

We hear about pain and suffering on a daily basis. All you have to do is turn on the news for a few minutes to see that we are a broken world full of broken people. Heartache, disease, and poverty plague our countries, cities, and homes. Some of us lead a blessed life where these trials are minimal. Some of us live in a bubble where we are blinded by our monotonous and easy days. Some of us may recognize the needs and act accordingly. We donate two cents here, and share a prayer there. Some of us go the extra mile and take trips into third world places. Some of us give strangers unconditional love. Some of us even dedicate our lives to greater causes, filling the holes where divots lie. Some of us react when our hearts feel a tug.

I've done well to suppress the question of "why?" This word can be powerful in a very dark way. Finding yourself saying it can lead to a place you don't want to find yourself. These past few months have tested my ability to question. In those brief moments where my guard is let down and doubt creeps in, I firmly ask God to intervene. It was hard in the beginning. It's always harder when you can't see the light. I am thankful those times have passed and I see more clearly the answers to "why?" I don't have to question because I know. I know our daughter was chosen to walk this path to bring people hope in times of trouble. I know I was given this journey for the purpose of endurance in faith. I know, without a shadow of doubt, our family was blessed to have this challenge. God saw an opportunity to show his love in a big way, and I stand in awe at his success.

Brooklyn's morning X-ray is a result of this success. It was remarkable. Her lungs are continuing to fill with air, and the effusions have started to fade. The doctors have written orders to increase her milk feeds to 13 cc's. Each decent X-ray will come with a bigger meal. This continued progression will hopefully lead toward the removal of her IV, and the discontinuing of TPN. Inch by inch, mile by mile, we will reach that finish line. Rose from OT came by earlier this morning to work with Brooklyn's oral feeding. There is still some concern regarding Brooklyn's ability to swallow. A study may need to be done in a few weeks to gauge this issue. Brooklyn needs to gain more control over her gag reflex in order to make mealtime more positive. The partially paralyzed vocal cord, and swollen glands, may be contributors to these hardships in swallowing. The throat exam in two weeks will give the team a better understanding of truth to this theory.

Some of us will experience angst and despair. Some of us will grow from these fears. Some of us will learn to put trust in prayer. Some of us will reap the rewards. Some of us will lean not on our understandings. Some of us will submit to the Lord. Some of us will find strength in our faith, and those will find peace in straight paths.

Home Stretch

Today was the first time a plan to go home had been brought up.

I almost lost my breath when Dr. W approached me with a time frame of how soon Brooklyn could be discharged. Brooklyn has never been the NICU kid that was lucky enough to have this conversation. The doctors have come to an agreement that Brooklyn will be ready in four weeks if she can nipple feed. If not, we are still only looking at eight weeks. If four weeks have come and gone without any luck at the feedings by mouth, a g-tube will need to be placed in Brooklyn's stomach. If a feeding tube is inserted, our visits to TCH will be frequent. Every three to four days the doctors will want to follow up with Brooklyn. Additional appointments will also be scheduled if her effusions come back. This compromise will let us bring our girl home instead of being inpatient for an extended amount of time.

As long as feedings continue to go well, and her X-rays look decent, Brooklyn will be weaned from the Octreotide. Our prayers are about to get real specific. We need Brooklyn's body to be clear of chylothorax without the help of medication. We need her oral aversions to dissipate. We need her gag reflex to subside, and her throat to be healed in order for swallowing to be successful. We need her to be able to digest full feeds without major issues. We need her to grow exponentially as nourishment is received by her body.

We need Brooklyn to finish the race.

She has come so far that we can finally see light at the end of the tunnel. It's her time to shine and let the whole world see the power of prayer. Please help us pray that God's mercy and grace be seen through this small child. Let her audience be witnesses to a miracle.

Thank you Lord for this incredible example of your love and grace.

Let Go

Brooklyn is doing well this morning. I arrived to catch the tail end of her PO feeding with Rose. She was squirming and highly perturbed, but actually wanting to take the bottle. Rose was telling me that her actions were showing us that she desires the bottle. Brooklyn's problem is that swallowing is a major challenge. Too much milk flow into her mouth causes an immediate gag or cough response, making it unpleasant to eat. It breaks your heart to see her want it so badly, only to get a little and choke.

Last night at small group the theme was bondage. We discussed certain areas in our lives where freedom is sought and chains need be broken. Insecurity, resentment, guilt, lies, and shame were a few words tossed around. For some, bondage is easily recognized. For others, perhaps not. Some of us may find that it takes true examination and reflection to determine certain obstacles that tie us down. Searching oneself is never easy and often comes with a cost. Wanting to change and successfully changing are two points that lie on opposite ends of a spectrum. Seeking liberty and being liberated are indeed two very different ideas.

Brooklyn's bondage is her oral aversion. Her mind allows her to believe that something in her mouth will cause pain and irritation. It associates the liquid going down her throat with the ventilation tube which no longer exists. Until she can realize that the milk is not meant to harm her, but free her, she will remain under this bondage. It's hard to change when you've been in chains for so long. Just as it will take time for Brooklyn's throat to heal, so it may take time for some us to heal.

As Christians, we are the prisoners and Jesus is our rescuer. He can set us free from any bondage we put ourselves in. I say "put" because it is by our own free will that we fall into the traps of being held captive. It is only by coming to God, and laying down our burdens, that we will be free.

Let go and let God.

Dance Shoes

Trust is having confidence in someone or something, even when you may not have foresight in the outcome. We rely on our intuition that what or who we are entrusting will not let us down. Trusting, is firmly believing that integrity exists.

When perfect strangers hear about Brooklyn and selflessly give in honor of her battle, they are trusting faith. I have been placed in a state of shock by others generosity. To find a check in our mailbox from a name we have never heard is proof of God's grace. My heart is overwhelmed by the many we have come to know through this experience. With each new friend, I find myself learning more about who God is and how he works. To be a part of this love equation gives me a feeling of elation.

Brooklyn is showing us new developments every day. One of the nurses had suggested we bring a play mat up to the hospital. Brooklyn has reached a point where sitting in a crib all day just doesn't cut it. Her lack of stimulation causes her to become irritable and anxious. I don't blame her, and if she is anything like her Mom, she won't be able to sit still long. If only she could speed up the feeding process we could go home and play all day.

Her mealtime last night left us feeling discouraged. She is still coughing whenever she tries to swallow. It's hard to fathom how something as natural as a swallow could be someone's nemesis. Whatever is not taken by mouth is put into a syringe and fed through Brooklyn's nose tube. They have put the milk on a one hour timer so that she doesn't have to tolerate one large amount at a time. This slow trickle will help her digest the food more easily. Brooklyn has done great with her residuals and less than frequent spit up's. Her body is showing us it's ready, but her mouth and throat are still in protest.

Once full feeds are reached, the Octreotide will be weaned. This is another huge hurdle Brooklyn will face. The chylothorax has been tamed all because of this medication given three times a day. Many breaths will be held as our girl is taken off this helping agent. Tomorrow brings another increase to Brooklyn's milk and one more step in the right direction. We thank God for her continued growth and perseverance. It is an indescribable feeling that our girl is on a faster track to coming home.

Covered in dust we pull out our dance shoes from the attic. As the weeks come and Brooklyn is healed, these shoes will be cleaned and polished. And on that day we take her home, we will put on our shoes, and dance for what the Lord has done.

3 Months

Brooklyn is three months old today. As she lies in her crib, grin on her face, I think to myself how lucky I am. From her head full of hair down to her monkey toes, she is perfect. I look around at her remaining attachments and thank God for how far she has come. We are only a few accessories away from bringing her home.

Brooklyn's morning X-ray showed no change. Her pleural effusions, if any, are minimal, and her lungs continue to be expanded. The picture looks good, so feeds will be increased to 33 cc's at 70 per kg. This is up from 22 cc's and 50 per kg. Both amount and volume will slowly rise until optimal nutrition is reached through breast milk. At that point, TPN can be discontinued and Brooklyn's central line can be removed.

There is a very real possibility of a g-tube, or gastrostomy tube. Brooklyn would undergo a simple procedure of inserting a button on her stomach. This will provide an alternative access to providing nutrition. Before we come home, Jered and I would learn how to administer Brooklyn's feedings through this tube. Once she is able to feed by mouth, the tube would be extracted. The doctors are planning to give her a few more weeks before setting a date to put in a g-tube. If Brooklyn can successfully take a bottle, we won't have to go down that road. During OT this morning, Rose admitted that Brooklyn is on a very slow pace as far as feedings are concerned. Although she sees improvement, there are still some strong aversions to overcome. Brooklyn may need more than a couple weeks to jump these hurdles.

Tomorrow brings a new month and a new set of doctors once again. I can't help but wonder if this team will be the last to treat Brooklyn. It's possible that by the end of this next month our little munchkin will be discharged. Regardless of whether this is true, a new set of eyes will be refreshing. I'm interested to see this new attending and his reputation of being "eye candy". There is a buzz around the unit as the nurses discuss his return to the rotation.

Happy 3 months little girl. Your Dad and I are proud of your fighting spirit. We can't wait to bring you home and show you off.

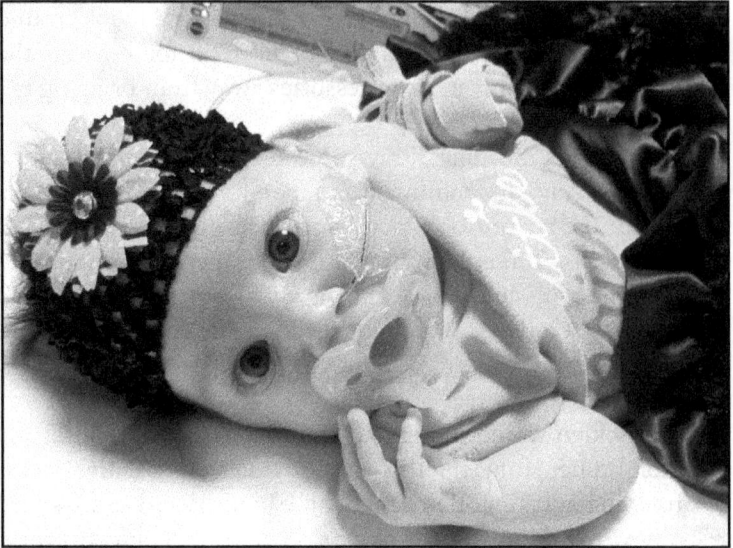

Tranquil Tuesday

Brooklyn made her Momma proud as she successfully sucked down 5 cc's of breast milk from her bottle this morning. She even got ahead of herself a couple times, taking the milk faster than her throat would allow. After a few coughs and gags, the OT had me force a pace. After two or three sucks I would pull the bottle out of her mouth and wait for her to swallow. Brooklyn didn't much mind us taking her food away. Too much milk and she gags, too little and she cries for more. I was just thrilled to see her actually wanting to take the bottle. I know it's only a matter of time before she gets the hang of it.

Brooklyn now weighs 8 pounds 7 ounces. You go girl! Slowly but surely she is working her way up the growth chart. Apart from the occasional spit up, she is able to digest her food well. She has adequately tolerated the increase in amount and volume, so they will continue the current plan as long as her X-rays look good. The nurse practitioner did say Brooklyn looked a bit swollen, but would just keep an eye out for other signs of reoccurring effusions. The X-ray scheduled for Thursday will hopefully rest our fears and everything will be normal.

I'm happy to say that things are a bit boring today. All is quiet and uneventful. I'll take a whole heap of these days without hesitation. It won't be a hot minute before the "crazy" kicks back in. I'm thankful for the days that allow me to breathe. I take advantage of the hours where I can prop my feet up and twiddle my thumbs. I thank God for this tranquil Tuesday.

Second Wind

Today was "get my life in order" day. After a visit to the bank, a meeting with the mailbox, dental cleaning, vision office drive by, and phone call to social security, I feel somewhat productive. I like putting all the things I hate to do in one day. That way it doesn't ruin my whole week, just a measly 12 hours.

I of course found time to squeeze in a visit to the NICU where my brave little toaster was trying her best at feeding. One projectile vomit and a couple heaves later, Brooklyn managed to hold down about 3 cc's. Hey, we'll take what we can get. Eating exhausted our girl and she slipped into a coma 15 minutes after the start of her meal. As always, the remaining milk was administered via her nose tube while she caught a few zzz's. Rose was pleased with the session and is encouraged. Here is to having faith that the coming weeks will bring significant momentum.

Dr. O made a surprise appearance at bedside today. He was very pleased to see how well Brooklyn is doing. We chatted a few minutes about the doctor's long term schedule and plan to go home. We discussed the possibility of Brooklyn's g-tube and what it would entail as far as reoccurring appointments were concerned. He encouraged me to be proactive in rounds, sharing my opinions about Brooklyn's progress in feeding. He reminded me how I as the mother have the best perception when it comes to Brooklyn's development. I have a "sixth sense" as you might say into which goals are attainable and which ones are not. His comment reminded me that now is not the time to slack off on being attentive to the little cues my daughter signals. These final weeks before coming home will be crucial to how well prepared we are. Being discharged does not automatically give Brooklyn a "get out of jail free" card. She will still have many obstacles to face with her homecoming.

I shall not become meek in spirit. Just as my daughter has proven her strength, so must I remain strong. God give me my "second wind". The sails in this ship still need a strong breeze.

Unmatchable

Memories from ECMO came rushing back as a child had to be put on the machine this morning. I still feel that pit in my stomach whenever the word is spoken. I know what that family is going through right now and I never want to feel that helpless again. Flashbacks of Brooklyn's lifeless body, covered in surgical dye still haunt me. I don't know the specifics of this infant's case, but my heart aches for the parents. That bleak four letter word is one of the monsters that hover over the NICU. You know it's there, lurking in the corner, but you tell yourself it's not coming after you. I lift this family up in prayer as they walk a similar road we took two months ago.

The back has been shut down due to this surgery, so I am out running errands. The nurse practitioner grabbed me before I left to tell me Brooklyn's X-ray looks great. The team will place an order to increase her feeds and possibly discuss coming off Octreotide. I was a little concerned with her high respiratory rate and heartbeat, but I didn't get a chance to ask the nurse about it. I will return this afternoon and be sure to mention it. It's remarkable how attuned I am to every detail of Brooklyn. How many breaths she takes per minute to the color of her skin. I make sure nothing abnormal gets by me.

As the week draws to an end I'm reminded of the time left before the doctors decide to put a g-tube in Brooklyn's belly. Her morning session went well, but Rose still believes she needs significant time before taking a full bottle of milk. I keep strong faith in my little girl, having hope she will show us her inspiring perseverance and unmatchable stubbornness to succeed. She knows how to stir a crowd, and I'm positive she still has a few tricks up her sleeve.

Brooklyn's Big Bash

The sky likes to open up and make the ground wet on big events our life.

Exhibit A: our wedding. For those of you who had the pleasure of attending our special day, you know all too well of the sauna fest. The rain combined with humidity had everyone looking like Albert Einstein. We made the best of it of course, and I wouldn't have wanted it any other way. My dress had a good foot and a half ring around the bottom, covered in mud. It was without a doubt one of the best parties I'd ever been involved in.

Now on to Exhibit B: Brooklyn's Benefit. I keep looking at the weather channel in hopes to hear a different forecast. So far, a consistent 60% chance of rain and thunderstorms still persists. I know whatever the clouds bring won't spoil our fun, but I really hope the rain doesn't discourage people from coming. I promise you will be shown a good time come rain or shine. I can't guarantee a beautiful hair day, but I can promise great food, awesome tunes, and good company. I really have been so excited to see everyone. The hospital has been somewhat of a prison at times, and I am more than ecstatic to get out and socialize. You can't ever go wrong when reuniting with old friends.

Brooklyn will unfortunately miss her big bash. Her day will be spent hanging out in the NICU with some of her favorite nurses. She has gone up to 38 cc's of milk, so she'll be working extra hard to keep her meals down. Saturdays are also bath days, so she will be enjoying "spa time". There's nothing like feeling clean and taking a long nap. I'm sure her day will be just fine. Speaking of nap, our girl has been out since I arrived this morning. I'm enjoying her odd positions as she tries to get comfortable. I could literally sit and stare at this wonderful creation all day.

In fact, I just might do that right now.

My Personal Genie

The benefit surpassed all of my expectations, and here I stand again, awestruck by others generosity.

We had an astonishing turnout yesterday. The weather started out quite brutal, but as the day went on, the sun showed us a little mercy. A couple tarps saved the afternoon and allowed the gruesome wind to stay at bay under the pavilion. It was amusing to see all us Texans dressed like Eskimos in the month of March. We've had some intense weather over the past few months and I think it's safe to say we are ready for the scorching heat that summer will bring. But really, the amount of support our family was shown was unbelievable. I am so thankful for old and new friends, family, and even strangers who felt the need to love on Brooklyn. We couldn't have asked for a better day.

Getting back to the hospital to see our rock star was the perfect ending. She has no idea the magnitude of inspiration she has created. She fights everyday without knowing she is a hero. Her life is similar to Jim Carrey's on that movie The Truman Show. Every detail of her day is put on display to show the world of God's unfailing love. Everyone wants to believe that miracles still exist. Brooklyn provides proof. Even as young children we are intrigued by things like "magic", and "genies". A quote I came across this week fits perfectly into this idea.

"Why wish upon a star when you can pray to the one who created it." -Annie Moore

This childlike sense that we "wish" for something good to happen is actually attainable through prayer. How awesome is that? Not to say that Jesus is our personal genie, but He is very capable of providing us the desires of our hearts. Granted, we often ask out of selfish gain or greedy tendencies, so I am thankful for unanswered prayer. But God sees our needs and will meet them as long as we remain faithful. He has proven time and again that He hears our pleas, and will continue to take action as we come to Him.

Brooklyn has supernatural favor upon her. I keep saying that her prayer warriors grow exponentially by the hour. Every time I hear of a new follower, I thank God for His work. He took one small story and created hope for His people. Brooklyn's parable is one that can reach anyone who has ever questioned faith or found themselves hopeless.

Never underestimate the power of prayer and God's grace. You will be surprised what faith the size of a mustard seed will produce.

Houston, We Have A Plan

Full feeds are finally here. Goodbye TPN, hello projectile vomiting.

Brooklyn is up to 58 cc's, or approximately 3 ounces of milk every three hours. This amount, plus its new volume, equal what Brooklyn should be taking based on her age and weight. The super nutrition, or TPN, has been discontinued. If by the end of the week our girl has no major hiccups, her central line will be taken out. This will be a tremendous victory on this demanding road. Brooklyn's PICC line has been in since the day she was born. With these IV's, there is always an increased risk of infection. As my hand knocks on wood, I whisper that it is a miracle Brooklyn was able to dodge this bullet. Her mighty immune system is one to be envied.

As we reach this milestone of full nutrition, tomorrow begins the weaning of her Octreotide. This is the medication that has supposedly been the main player in keeping Brooklyn's chylothorax tamed. The doctors believe we have cleared the time period of concern with accumulated fluid. As cases in the past have presented, an extended absence of the perfusions indicates they have dissipated. However, because there is not a significant amount of evidence to prove Octreotide's effectiveness, there is no protocol on the weaning process. Expert opinions will be brought in from pharmacy to discuss the next step. Since Brooklyn is not receiving the medication on a drip, a percentage of the dose will need to be cut. Past research and literature will also be analyzed to help determine this calculation.

Rose sat in on rounds this morning to give her advice on Brooklyn's long term feeding plan. She let the team of doctors know that it will be a long road, and a g-tube will inevitably need to be inserted. Rose feels that the sooner this tube goes in, the sooner Brooklyn can come home. Nurse Michelle is completely on board as well and encouraging the decision. Away from the NICU, our girl will be less likely to catch any bug lurking around her neighbors. Dr. R wants to give her a few more weeks to declare herself and then a g-tube will be considered. The sooner we get that tube, the faster our exit will be.

I arrived this morning to catch PT working with Brooklyn. It's rare that I'm here while they perform her exercises, so I took the opportunity to chat about her progress. After a 40 minute session with her, they made a determination that Brooklyn is only about one month behind developmentally. I am very happy with this news. The therapist went on to say that her head and neck control are getting stronger, and she is using her stomach muscles more every time. They continued to provide me some easy positions to try without them. She needs more tummy time to practice lifting and rotating her head. I think we can handle this simple request.

As we get closer to Brooklyn's homecoming, our "checklist" grows. Jered and I are in the process of scheduling our CPR training. We will also be learning about the g-tube, and how each feeding session will go. Fortifying Brooklyn's milk will be done at home, so we will also be learning how to do this on our own. Brooklyn will have several appointments each month at Texas Children's to see specialists. These outpatient visits include one to the GI department to monitor Brooklyn's abdomen. She will also need a regular pediatrician near our home that feels comfortable taking a former CDH child.

Jered and I are slowly becoming quite proficient in our nursing skills. Although there will be challenges at home, I feel prepared to handle what may come. Butterflies dance in my stomach at the thought of not having our nurses at her side, but I'm confident in the abilities we've acquired. It's hard to think you can miss a place that has so many painful memories, but the staff has become like family to us. Each day Brooklyn grows stronger is a reminder that we will not be here forever. The word "bittersweet" twirls in my mind as I picture the day we will say goodbye.

Just Keep Swimming

Today was initiation day.

To celebrate Brooklyn's 100th day of life, she decided to poop on me. Boy was that a hoot. There she was, innocently sitting on my lap, when all of a sudden, a rumble emerged down below. Brooklyn's face turned sour, a sure sign that something unpleasant just took place in her diaper. Reaching down to check the damage, I grazed my pants. Warm goo. It was confirmed at this point that Brooklyn's diaper had exploded. Poop was everywhere. Picking her up, I carried her to the bed like a bag full of stink bait, and as far away from my body as possible. I swear I saw the girl grin as I removed her soiled underpants.

Brooklyn continued to have stomach issues throughout the afternoon. Luckily, none were as catastrophic and thankfully contained. Michelle reminded me that it was probably what I ate that was making Brooklyn's tummy go bonkers. Everything I take to mouth affects my breast milk, and then gets transferred to Brooklyn. Her little belly was not appreciating the obvious Mexican meal I devoured on December 15th. I need to keep her in mind when Dad wants pizza every other night. If she's like her Momma, grease doesn't do our sensitive stomachs any favors.

As Brooklyn's stomach talked to us all day, the doctors decided to hold on any changes to her care. The milk drip is currently on 130 ml's per kilo, and is running continuously. The team thought it a good idea to feed slowly so that Brooklyn would not be so uncomfortable. She has yet to get use to the voluminous intake, and it will take time for her body to adjust. Decreasing the speed of milk flow will hopefully help with reflux and spit up's. Her Octreotide has also been chopped in half. Tomorrow they will cut the dose down to once every twelve hours in hopes to discontinue it by Friday.

Good. One less thing.

Monica is back tonight so I have a feeling our girl has her personal DVD player again. Last night Brooklyn watched Finding

Nemo before hitting the hay. Our girl's more rotten than a bag of old tomatoes. It's almost entertaining to see how many nurses she can get wrapped around her little finger. If nothing else, Brooklyn continues to hang in there as the days roll on by. Perhaps she's taken on Dori's philosophy and "just keeps swimming".

Forward March

———————

Brooklyn is pulling out her feeding tube an average of two times a day. She outsmarts even the craftiest of tape jobs. Finding the smallest loophole, she will sneak a finger in and quickly pull. The g-tube is looking pretty magnificent at this point. Her poor nose is so raw from the countless times the tube has been reinserted. Not to mention her cheeks are broken out from the DuoDerm and tape to keep the tube in place. Dr. R wants to give her another week and a half before putting the g-tube in. I'm all for giving her a chance, but it's going to take more than a few weeks to get her taking full feeds from a bottle. Maybe I'll be proven wrong, but I sure like the sound of coming home.

I don't know what has caused my sense of urgency, but the past couple of days I've been abnormally anxious. I think it has a lot to do with Ella being discharged this coming Tuesday. It also may have a bit to do with how well Brooklyn is doing. She wants to get up and play, socialize, and entertain people. Even her bouncer is too boring for her. I keep thinking back to the time she was sensitive to the slightest touch or sound. Now it's like she needs a rollercoaster to be tamed.

On my list of to do's this afternoon included interviewing Brooklyn's pediatrician. Texas Children's Physicians Association has a Pearland clinic that currently takes Medicaid. After reviewing the doctors online, I decided to schedule a meeting with Dr. V. I was highly impressed with her knowledge about CDH. Although the office has only had one child with this condition, Wendy seemed very competent in the issues they often struggle with. She asked all the right questions, and I felt confident with her ability to treat Brooklyn. She gave me a tour of the facility and introduced me to her job partner and nursing staff. Their kindness made me feel like family, and I am certain they will provide excellent care for our girl. Unfortunately, Jered is working out of town and wasn't able to make the appointment. But I'm sure he would have been impressed by their hospitality and educational background.

Brooklyn's Octreotide has been weaned to one dose every 12 hours. Friday we will say our goodbyes to this drug and give a fond farewell to Brooklyn's central line. One less wire to deal with. Prevacid has been ordered to help with reflux, but this can be given by mouth. Any extra medications or vitamins from here on out will be administered orally.

The next two weeks will challenge my patience as we wait to hear news about a g-tube. I'm ready to move forward but must remember it is not my timing. Brooklyn leads the way as we come face to face with the next leg of this road. She sets her pace as the rest of us file in. Brooklyn is our commanding officer as we take orders for this march.

Left, left, left right left.

New Plan

Brooklyn's central line has been removed. Every nurse that has cared for her is celebrating this monumental event. The fact that this line has been in since admission without infection is astounding. Brooklyn's immune system has proven itself worthy of taking on this battle. If there were a trophy for MVP, it would have gone home with recognition. With the exit of this IV, Brooklyn is down to one feeding tube and two monitors. Apart from the frequent heaving, our girl is very content. My hope is that the Prevacid her doctors have prescribed will take effect to Brooklyn's reflux problem.

Standing by Brooklyn's bed this afternoon, I overheard her physicians talking about her homecoming. Apparently Brooklyn's abdominal anatomy is not compatible with the g-tube. Her upper GI examination convinced the surgeons that an NG tube is more suitable for her feedings. This is the nose tube that connects to a syringe providing a continuous flow of milk. Jered and I will learn how to insert the tube and check for its proper placement. Unfortunately, Brooklyn finds enjoyment from pulling this tube out. I'd hate to think our girl will need to wear socks on her hands until she's able to eat by mouth, but this may be the case.

Going home with the NG tube means two things;

1. No surgery, and
2. Our discharge date gets pushed up.

Bring on the anxiety attacks ….

I am more than ready to see Brooklyn come home, but at the same time I'm nervous to be nurse and doctor free. We have had the greatest babysitters of all time. To go from expert care to Jered and I is a tad overwhelming. Fear sets in as I think of the nights I will lie awake, listening intently to every stir Brooklyn makes. Blood pressure medicine should be a requirement for NICU parents as they exit the hospital.

No exact date has been set for our discharge as of yet. Jered and I still need to take CPR and training sessions on how to manage the NG tube. I'm sure a checklist is on its way to help us be confident in Brooklyn's release. I can feel the Lord's presence upon me as I prepare for the next turn in this road. Brooklyn has taken the path less traveled, and I'm certain she will continue this pattern. I'm grateful for the extra patience God has granted me to take on this challenge. Without his calming hand on my shoulder, this journey may have taken a different turn.

Allowing myself to fully trust in Him has made all the difference.

Bravo

Causing your child pain, whether intended or not, will always inadvertently break your spirit. As I watch the nurse reinsert Brooklyn's nose tube for the ump-tenth time, I cringe. Her tiny body flails and her poor face scours in agony as pressure is forced upon her red nostril. It's bad enough that I have to watch the nurse do this. How am I supposed to be ok with shoving a hard plastic object down my daughter's nose and into her stomach? How could anyone be ok with that?

I guess the answer is I have to be ok with it. Without this tube Brooklyn cannot eat. Without this tube she cannot grow. Without this tube she cannot survive. So regardless of how hard it is for the two of us, I must move on. I must be strong and give my daughter her lifeline. I just wish she knew I wasn't doing this to cause her discomfort. I cannot express enough how much I hope she starts taking a bottle well. My heart hums this morning for her throat to heal quickly, her reflux to dissipate, and feeding by mouth becomes a realistic possibility. Until that point comes, my heart also hums for her wandering hands. That she would get familiar with the NG tube and not feel the need to tug so vigorously at it.

If there was one particular item that ignites my jealously with other NICU families it would be the car seat. Every parent knows that when the nurse asks you to bring the carrier in to be tested, your child is nearly free. My heart skipped a beat last night when our nurse requested that we bring the seat in the next time we come. The doctors make sure that this purchased item passes regulation. They also want to ensure that your child doesn't drop his or her stats when being placed in the seat. The process is similar to a dog crate. You can't just toss a puppy into a new kennel and expect complete contentment. First, you must get them acquainted. Perhaps you even toss a treat in as mild bribery. I'm 90% sure Brooklyn will ease through the test, but we'll have some strawberry blow pops on hand just in case.

Nurse Michelle is in for a surprise on Monday. Like the rest of us, she left for the week in anticipation for the g-tube. Once again Brooklyn has pulled a fast one on us. You would think by now we'd be use to these little charades. However, we sit again dumbfounded by Brooklyn's trickery. I know good and well there is a reason Brooklyn is keeping the NG tube. Perhaps God's plan is a little more intricate than we had thought. He knows the story before it is told and I'm more confident in His version than ours. Maybe He knows the g-tube isn't necessary, and soon our girl will begin eating. Or what if God knows Brooklyn better than we do and feels this path is better?

I'm leaning toward the last one and KNOW that God knows better. I will not debate His wisdom. He has lined up each stanza in this extended poem perfectly. He is putting final touches on His masterpiece in hopes to wow us one more time.

Bravo Jesus for intervening when we humans fail to see what's best.

Royalty

We have much to be thankful for today. Above all else, we are thankful for the gift of life. Watching Vito's family have to say goodbye last night put everything into perspective again. My eyes began to tear as the nurse placed his tiny feet onto an ink pad, and then pressed them against white card-stock. His Mom was being so brave yet broken in the same instant. This is an all too familiar feeling among NICU parents. Yes, we have much to be thankful for today. We are thankful for God's gift in Brooklyn's life.

Its visitation Monday as family strolls in from out of town. The beginning of Spring Break has shown its face. Brooklyn's great aunt Miriam heads this way with her niece. Gigi will be here as well to capture the new meet and greet. Aunt Jennifer will most likely swing by as she takes a break from her kiddos at school. I'm not a teacher, but I can only assume that this week long break is undoubtedly necessary for their sanity.

Today I will learn how to insert Brooklyn's nose tube, check residuals, and administer her medications. Only the first of these has me wanting to crawl into a cave. I know I will be able to do it, I just don't know how willing I will be. What I am most afraid of is becoming a pro at reinserting the tube. As Brooklyn grows more each day, her intelligence increases. She is more aware that something unpleasant is going down one of her pipes. She has become particularly sneaky in reaching that pointer finger exactly where the tube comes out. She will rest her small finger on her nose and wait, look around like; "What? This is where I rest my finger." Sure you do sweetheart. Then the minute I turn my back the tube is lying in the bed, dripping milk onto the sheets.

Brooklyn's last weight was measured at 3900 grams, or 8 pounds 9 ounces. The doctors are still concerned that her growth trend is not sufficient. CDH babies are well known for their inability to gain weight at a normal rate. The reason for this is their fast respiratory rates and reflux issues. Diaphragmatic Hernia babies breathe faster than the average child because of how their lungs began. With space compromised in their chest at the beginning, they have to work harder to bring air into their lungs. Reflux is another annoyance they face due to the shifting of their anatomy. Although it should clear over time, this hindrance will cause spit up's and loss of calories.

A tentative date of March 28th has been set for Brooklyn's homecoming. There are only a few loose ends to tie up. Michelle wants to be on staff for our discharge date, and the 28th looks promising. We will discuss with the doctors to make sure this time works for all parties involved. I'm still in disbelief that we get to take our daughter home in just a few days. It won't be real until we carry her out in the car seat. Smiles on our faces, and scared out of our minds, we will embark on new territory.

Bringing our princess to her castle is almost here. We may not have a chariot that awaits her departure, but I'm positive this Diva will rule the royal headquarters.

One Roof

Brooklyn is getting her days and nights in order. This will be extremely beneficially come next Wednesday when we take her home. Yes, you read correctly, WEDNESDAY!

After rounds yesterday morning, the doctors officially set our discharge date to Wednesday. Jered, Brooklyn, and I will stay the night at TCH Tuesday for a "trial run". We will be staying in one of their designated family rooms as a test before we can go home. As long as no major catastrophe's strike, we will be allowed to take Brooklyn home. Miss Ella Rose had her stay last night, so we say goodbye to our dear friend this morning. As I watch Emma and James pack Ella's things, jitter bugs fight in my stomach. We will be doing this same thing in only 8 days.

Brooklyn is snoozing this morning. She's somewhat of a late sleeper, which by the way, I'm totally on board with. However, I must give credit where it's due because she acquired this from her Dad's side. I won't name names because they know who they are, but there are a few sleeping beauties who like their shut eye. As Brooklyn rests her eyes, I go over the checklist with our nurse again. CPR training is tomorrow at 1 o'clock, shortly after our walk thru of our new house.

Oh did I forget to mention we bought a house?

Not only did we buy a house, we close on the same day Brooklyn is released. Can we please make life a little more insane? We are still hammering out the details on how this will all go down. There is no plan as of yet, and frankly, I'm nervous to try and even jot one down. I'm sure we will make it all work out, but really, if you see my head rolling down the street, don't be alarmed. I'll be running right behind it trying to put myself together.

CPR Training, NG tube placement for Jered, car seat class, food pump exercises, and feed mixing lessons are still to be completed. We will be going home on part breast milk, part formula, so I will need to learn measurements for these. There will also be a discussion about medications and how to administer

Brooklyn's Prevacid. For the remainder of our time in the NICU, I will be Brooklyn's primary nurse. I will do assessments, check residuals, and give feeds and medication. Come next week there will be nothing I can't handle. As long as we don't push the panic button during our overnight stay, we will be home free. Yes, there is a panic button. Hopefully it won't look to tempting as we brave the night alone.

Before my life becomes booked and I'm housebound, today is deemed shopping day. My Mom is picking me up at noon and we are going to paint the town. I plan on enjoying the heck out of this last bit of freedom. This next week is going to be one for the books. I couldn't think of a better scenario than bringing Brooklyn into our brand new home. Finally our life can begin. We can start our family the way it is intended, sleeping and eating under one roof.

Humble Endurance

Brooklyn had to throw one last punch before her big send-off could take place.

The follow-up ultrasound to check the status of a small blood clot in Brooklyn's abdomen was supposed to be routine and uneventful. Brooklyn didn't agree. Where the 1 centimeter thrombus once sat now lies a 5 centimeter clot. Because the growth is so significant, hematology has stepped in to suggest treatment. Brooklyn will now go home on a blood thinner called Lovenox. This drug is fairly safe and only has a small risk of altering platelet levels and bleeding. The not so good news is I will have to give my daughter a shot every 12 hours for the next 3-6 months....

Delightful.

If all goes according to plan, our release date will still be next Wednesday. Jered and I will be taught how to administer the Lovenox injections as soon as possible. If we both feel comfortable with all of Brooklyn's requirements, she will be discharged. CPR training has been completed as of 2 o'clock this afternoon. The class was your average public skills session which always includes a common item; the "let's be obnoxious" guy. I mean really, who stands up an infant CPR doll and walks it across the table making robot sounds? The class is merely an hour long. Is it too much to ask to keep the crazy locked up for 60 minutes? Nevertheless, we all received our green certificates by the end of class. I'm very thankful the hospital provides this service. I feel more at ease knowing how to handle a situation where, heaven forbid, my child is unconscious.

Nurse Michelle was joking as she asked me if I had prayed for patience. After confirming her suspicion, she mentioned that it's never a good idea to ask for patience unless you are willing to bear situations that call for it. God has a remarkable way of teaching patience through firsthand experience. He may not give you more than you can handle, but He won't shy away from pushing the limits. I consider myself competent of the ability to be patient, but perhaps I need a refresher. Our new "needle assignment" will reinforce my humble endurance. It will challenge both perseverance and stamina. My only choice is to be bold, taking on the challenge with a light heart.

I will stand firm on the ground of faith, knowing that this too shall pass.

Will You Follow

The past few days have felt a bit like the scene in Home Alone where the family is racing through the airport. The song, "Run, Run, Rudolph" plays in the background as chaos ensues.

Brooklyn will receive Lovenox injections twice daily for a minimum of three months. It's only been a few days and her legs are already bruising. Jered and I will alternate turns being the bad guy while the other tries to not cry. We are hopeful that the routine will become easier, but for now, 9 o'clock is a dreaded hour. I will attend a 30 minute session on Monday about the Lovenox drug. Hematology will be coming by shortly after to discuss how the medication will come, and what preparation will be required.

The medical supplies team dropped off our portable pump and all of the feeding equipment yesterday evening. The distributor gave a short demonstration of how the pump operates and what will be necessary for travel. Because Brooklyn is on continuous feeds, I'm pretty sure the front yard is about the furthest distance we will travel for a while. Until I get the hang of everything and set a schedule, Brooklyn and I plan on enjoying the confines of our new home.

With the delivery of our supplies, the reality of what is happening hit. The days have flown by with all loose ends being tied. I've neglected updates only because my days have been a blur. This whirlwind has me realizing my extracurricular hobbies are about to come to a halt. Brooklyn coming home will undoubtedly alter my daily routine. Taking the hospital out of my equation both excites and frightens me. My role as unemployed housewife is about to transform like Optimus Prime. No longer will I be the bedside observer, but an involved and attentive Mother/nurse. Brooklyn is relying on me to help her finish strong in this saga, and I refuse to be idle. Instead, I listen intently to the tasks I will be responsible for at home. The back of the car seat safety sheet is my wingman. I've jotted down the times, doses, and particulars of each drug and feed Brooklyn will come home on. There is no other option than to be prepared.

As I sit here and type, I feel a sense of closure emerging. Brooklyn has finally reached the end of her stay in the NICU, and the farewell is humbling. Her story has not only redefined my faith, but has opened my eyes to a new definition of community. How a small child can stir an army has truly been an inspiration. Her fight has taught us that God will provide if we are diligent in faith. Our family has experienced the power of prayer firsthand. From day one of learning about Brooklyn's diagnosis, our eyes have seen the hand of God. Through our daughter's journey, we have witnessed miracles. Even in the midst of adversity and setbacks, our girl has persevered. With each hurdle she clears, I stand in amazement at God's grace. He continues to show us how, even when our eyes see trials ahead, His plan will overcome and be revealed. There has been no better feeling than watching a broken sinner rejoice in His name due to finding God's mercy in Brooklyn's journey. Her tiny hand has reached even the desperate of hearts.

I will forever be grateful for Brooklyn's support group. Her followers kept my spirits high and encouraged my continued optimism. The prayer count our girl received was monumental. I am a firm believer that Brooklyn's healing was the result of intercession by those who believed in her restoration. By true confidence in God's unlimited love, we have succeeded.

Brooklyn is coming home.

I want to express my gratitude again for all the help our family received during the past four months. My heart is filled with appreciation as I reflect on the contributions and sacrifices that were made. For those of you who have been here every day to follow Brooklyn, her journey is far from over.

Brooklyn is my hero, my strength, and my life. It has been my honor to share her with you. As I draw to a close, I have but one charge;

God has moved. Will you follow?

March 24, 2011

The night before last I won a staring contest with a crib. The fact that the crib is made of wood, I consider myself unbeatable. Every flinch Brooklyn made was another jump out of bed. Apart from the occasional stir, she slept the whole night through. If only I could say the same for myself. If it wasn't the feeding pump waking me up, it was my nerves. Every ounce of me was on high alert. Nothing was going to take place without my knowledge, and nothing did. I heard every peep this chick muttered. Let's just say it'll be close to impossible for her to sneak out a window at 16.

Bringing Brooklyn home has been one of the most exhilarating, terrifying, and unbelievably rewarding experiences of my life. Leaving the hospital was surreal. My heart fluttered as we placed her in the back seat. At that moment I wanted to cover the entire car in bubble wrap. The freeway was a danger zone. People were driving way too fast and reckless. If there had been a back road to take to Needville, we would have been on it. I'm very proud to say that I only pulled over three times before meeting our destination. Operation "keep the pacifier in" was tough work. Brooklyn was a champ as usual and fell asleep in her seat. If it weren't for torn up roads and construction chaos, the trip would have been without pit stops. Regardless, our God was good to us as we made it safely home.

It was incredibly tough to leave our NICU family. A piece of my heart will forever be locked inside those unit walls. TCH has been our home for the past four months, and it is truly bittersweet to part from the building on Fannin. We will never forget Brooklyn's nurses Michelle and Monica. Their dedication to her care is something we will cherish forever. As I sit for a brief moment and reflect on her stay, I'm once again taken aback by the medical staff that supported Brooklyn's recovery. These people have a God given gift of compassion and patience. Some of the nurses may say that this was not their intended career path. I say God knew what He was doing when placing them there. It takes a great amount of strength to do what these individuals do, and I am eternally grateful for their desire to care. One of your rights as a patient being discharged is to make one last walk thru around the unit. I was the proudest Mom as I pushed Brooklyn in her stroller. With each face we said goodbye to, a memory would flash in my mind. We had waited for this day for so long, and it has finally shown itself.

No more monitors, no more alarms. Brooklyn's chains have been broken, and she has been set free. Her ransom has been paid by our Mighty God. Mercy poured upon a child. Unfailing love. Unending grace.

Afterword

182 days. 26 weeks. Half a year. 6 months. It doesn't matter how I write it, or how I say it, my mind can't comprehend it. Brooklyn is too small, too new, and too precious to already be this old.

Like all Moms I suppose, I want to stop time. I want to take the batteries out of my watch and make the second hand stand still. I want to keep these little moments, her tiny smile, forever. The thought of her growing up brings tears to my eyes. Not because I don't want to see her grow into a beautiful young lady, but because I can't bear to lose her innocent charm. She is completely perfect in every way. From her raspy growl to her chubby knees, she is beautiful. I look at her and see hope. Her life is proof of faith in action. Brooklyn isn't just a miracle; she is a reflection of steadfast prayer. She is a daily reminder that we are more than flesh and bones. Her story brings to life the soul inside me that reaches past the stars. The part of me that knows where home truly is; a place that celebrates forever. As she passes this small moment in time, I pause. I take in who she is and how she started. I remember the climb that led us to this place and how it has shaped our family. I place my finger in her little palm and thank God for all he has done. I pray for the next six months.

I wanted to make sure I acknowledged this milestone. Sure it's only six months, and while I'm positive there are the few who think I'm nuts, it doesn't matter. My sweet girl is growing up too fast to not make a big deal out of the small things. I want to celebrate every smile, and throw a party for each laugh. I want to dote over the best thing I ever made. Soon she will be all grown up, rolling her eyes when I tell her she's beautiful. So forgive me if I want to cherish her youth.

Life is short and I plan to live in each minute. Stopping if need be to remember the good times, learn from the bad, and give thanks for everything in between. God has given me such a fine life. There will be days I forget this, but that's what forgiveness is all about. We take things for granted, take wrong turns, and make a mess of things. Let's just be grateful for God's sense of humor and His unconditional love.